The Bones Reassemble

Reconstituting Liturgical Speech

Contemporary Religious Thought

Clayton Crockett and Jeffrey Robbins
Series Editors

This series publishes original works dealing with cutting-edge theoretical ideas in the field of religious studies and theology. A focused, interdisciplinary approach to religion is encouraged, an approach that will develop concepts and images in transformative ways, through engagement with disciplines and approaches such as Continental philosophy, semiotics, cultural studies, feminism, anthropology, psychology, sociology, political science, and the media.

Manuscript submissions are invited that are distinguished by their originality and creativity, rigorous scholarship, and an ability to communicate complex concepts with clarity and expressiveness. Younger scholars, especially, are encouraged to submit their work to this series. Proposals should be directed to Clayton Crockett and Jeffrey Robbins, Series Editors, The Davies Group Publishers, PO Box 440140, Aurora, Colorado, 80044-0140.

Carl A. Raschke, *The End of Theology*
Theresa Sanders, *Body and Belief*
Gabriel Vahanian, *Anonymous God*
Charles E. Winquist, *The Surface of the Deep*
Jeffrey W. Robbins, *In Search of a Non-Dogmatic Theology*
Gabriel Vahanian, *Tillich and the New Religious Paradigm*
Leonardo Messinese, *The Problem of God in Modern Philosophy*
Catherine Madsen, *The Bones Reassemble*

The Bones Reassemble

Reconstituting Liturgical Speech

Catherine Madsen

The Davies Group, Publishers   Aurora, Colorado

The author and publisher are grateful for permission to reprint from the following copy-righted material:

Lavon Bayler, "The Heavens Shout." From *Led by Love: Worship Resources for Year B*, (Cleveland: The Pilgrim Press, 1996), 205. Copyright 1996 by United Church Press. Used by permission.

Lavon Bayler , "Life Ebbs Away." From *Led by Love: Worship Resources for Year B*, (Cleveland: The Pilgrim Press, 1996), 217. Copyright 1996 by United Church Press. Used by permission.

"Holy and Good is the Gift of Desire" and "Eagles' spiralings comply." Words: Thomas H. Troeger (born 1945). From *New Hymns for the Life of the Church*, © 1992 Oxford University Press, Inc. Used by permission. All rights reserved.

"Reflections," by Rabbi Stanley Rabinowitz with adaptations by Rabbis Shamai Kanter and Jack Reimer, reprinted from the *Mahzor for Rosh Hashanah and Yom Kippur*, edited by Rabbi Jules Harlow, ©1972 by the Rabbinical Assembly, p. 228.

Sabbath Prayer Book, originally published 1945 by the Jewish Reconstructionist Founda-tion and *Kol Haneshamah: Shabbat Vehagim*, published by the Reconstructionist Press, Elkins Park, PAS, copyright 1994, sixth printing 2002. Used by permission.

Miriam Therese Winter, *WomanPrayer, WomanSong: Resources for Ritual*. Oak Park, Ill.: Meyer-Stone, 1987. Used by permission.

Cover art: Sarah E. Thomson, "How the Bones Grow." Watercolor, 2004. All rights reserved. Used by permission.

Library of Congress Cataloging-in-Publication Data

Madsen, Catherine, 1952-
    The bones reassemble : reconstituting liturgical speech / Catherine Madsen.
        p. cm.
    Includes bibliographical references (p.   ) and index.
    ISBN 1-888570-84-9 (alk. paper)
    1. Liturgical language--English. 2. English language--Religious aspects--
Christianity. 3. English language--Religious aspects--Judaism. I. Title.
    BV178.M33 2005
    264'.001'4--dc22

                                                                    2005005522

Contents

This book differs from other recent titles on modern liturgy in being neither a lament for a lost orthodoxy nor a quasi-technical manual for the home ritualist, but an analysis of what may be called the cognitive sources of strong liturgical language. Much of the widespread sense that nonfundamentalist religion is not "real" religion comes from the failure of recent revisions to produce coherent and compelling liturgy; I think the failure was not inevitable and need not be permanent. My investigations arose not from a professional commitment to theology or pastoral work, but from the pragmatic interest of a lay person in search of a religion worth practicing at a time when religious people seemed to have become exhausted with both their practice and their prose. The liturgists who set the tone for the revisions were simply concerned with using contemporary English; I am interested in the capacity of contemporary English for spiritual force.

I do not speak from any reflexively conservative stance. For reasons both personal and intellectual I am unassimilable to any orthodoxy, and have no objection in principle to radically altered or altogether new liturgy. I came to religion envying and desiring the beauty and gravity that recent liturgists have worked so hard to eliminate, but I know well enough that orthodoxy is no guarantor of moral insight and heterodoxy is no obstacle to it. Nor am I quite on the side of those who call for "the return of religion to public discourse" as a cure for social decay. Liturgy can influence the *level* of public discourse — its honesty, its intelligence, its ability to know a moral problem when it sees one — but the process is circuitous, and has less to do with a statement's overt moral or theological content than with the level of its introspection. People who want religion in public discourse think religion is good for you; I think, with Mary

McCarthy, that religion is only good for good people. I do suspect that the collapse of moral courage in liberal religion, and the general weakness of liberal politics after the Civil Rights Movement, devolved partly from the incapacity of liberal liturgists to confront moral crisis powerfully enough in language. One of my friends is fond of saying that "the Right is narrow, the Left is shallow"; I hope for a time when no one is willing to be either.

Few lay people in my position feel there is any point in protesting; they simply walk out of the service in a fury of insulted intelligence, or switch off their minds, or gravitate toward orthodox liturgies on a slight preference for narrowness over shallowness. There may be some use in standing one's ground. Not having been acculturated to any religion at a young age, I have no incentive to be tactful: modern liturgists — perhaps embarrassed by their own vestigial attachment to religion — have consistently underestimated their audience. In a culture where complex medical terminology is common currency and we all face any number of natural and political threats, it can be safely assumed that ordinary people can handle complexity in matters of life and death. Liturgical language is a public trust, and its moral and aesthetic problems reach farther than the circle of active religious practitioners; they touch everyone who comes to religion at a time of crisis as a source of credible help. The heavier the aesthetic cost of worship — the less it provides fit occupation for the mind and the emotions and the will — the more likely worshipers are to conclude that it means nothing even to its leaders, or else to accept the potentially lethal fundamentalist premise that serious worship entails insularity and rage. I have no right to set myself up as an authority — I'm nobody! who are you? — but if learned and qualified people have left it to an unevenly educated and morally dubious lay person to insist that liturgical writing is first of all writing, they cannot complain if she shows a certain impatience.

In the thirty or so years that liturgical questions have preoccupied me I have deliberately stayed on the margins of the academy.

Traditional disciplinary approaches preemptively cut off the very thing necessary for live liturgy — in religious studies the aesthetic and cognitive bedrock of language, in literary studies the compulsion toward worship in groups. Instead I have maintained the traditional lay distance from authorities with a system, and employed the quintessential lay method: scavenging, synthesis, the construction of my own understanding from voracious and not always systematic reading. I have found relatively little useful work in liturgical studies on the question of prose style, but there is so much that is relevant elsewhere that I have increasingly felt the synaptic overload of working with too much evidence. I feel a certain diffidence, not toward clergy and liturgists — exasperation is a great leveler — but toward scholars firmly situated in the disciplines I have drawn from; I hope my use of their work is not inaccurate or opportunistic.

Because I know Jewish liturgy most intimately, as a convert and an active lay leader for fifteen years, many of my examples will be drawn from Jewish sources; although liturgy in English is my central concern, examples in Hebrew can serve to illustrate certain phonetic points and principles of translation. From an earlier attempt at Christianity I also know the Anglican Book of Common Prayer well (I observed the transition from the old version to the new) and have investigated other Christian traditions to some extent. Garry Wills, Mary Gordon and others have represented the Catholic critique better than I could hope to, and I will not cover that ground. But much the same stylistic shift has occurred in Catholic, Protestant and liberal Jewish liturgies over the last several decades, and I intend the discussion to apply to the full range.

I would be remiss not to mention that fragments of substantive modern liturgy do exist. For readers looking for somewhere to begin, Leonard Cohen's *Book of Mercy*, Janet Morley's *All Desires Known*, and David Blumenthal's *Facing the Abusing God* will provide some sense of the possibilities. Certain poems, or sections of poems — by Richard Wilbur, Alicia Ostriker, Wendell Berry and others — can function liturgically; some of Yehuda Amichai's poems are already in liturgical use among secular Israelis, a promising development since Amichai's ironic use of traditional liturgical phrases keeps them in circulation. In a limited sense the *Shoah* has given rise to Jewish liturgies of mourning and Christian liturgies of repentance, the best of them extracanonical; David Roskies' *Night Words*, a finely literate *bricolage* of prose and verse, is the only one I know of that reads like liturgy rather than interfaith dialogue. But *all* the best work is extracanonical; it has little or no influence on official prayer books and provides no comprehensive substitute.

I am indebted to many people for direct and indirect help. The Association for Religion and Intellectual Life selected me for a Coolidge Fellowship in 1997; St Deiniol's Library in Hawarden, North Wales, and the Massachusetts Center for Renaissance Studies provided congenial places for research and writing. Mara Benjamin showed me Buber and Rosenzweig's essays on biblical translation, and Jay Ladin told me to read Lev Vygotsky and Stanley Fish; both these friends have provided critical intellectual sustenance even at wide intervals of time and space. David Daniell's interest in the book has meant a great deal to me, since his work on William Tyndale first convinced me that a lone dissident could make a difference. Rabbi Sheila Peltz Weinberg responded with grace as the humble and grateful proselyte grew into her Jewish inheritance and turned stiff-necked; Rabbi David Dunn Bauer provided proof that an artist's training is a high asset in liturgical work. Mark Doty, Alec Irwin, Jane Crosthwaite, Joseph Williamson, Joan Lindeman, Rafael Chodos, and Rabbi Dov Taylor each gave me the chance to test my ideas with undergraduates, graduate students, scholars, congregants, or colleagues. I am grateful for the conversation and encouragement of Judith Anderson, Rachel Barenblat, Linda Bills, Aaron Bousel, Rabbi William Cutter, Arnold Eisen, Chapman Flack, Paul Giurlanda, Rabbi Jill Hammer, Thomas and Winifred Madsen, Phyllis and Archie Nahman, Sean Norton, Barbara Thomson, Peter Willis, and my colleagues at *CrossCurrents*, particularly Scott Holland. I thank Aaron Lansky and my colleagues at the National Yiddish Book Center for their flexibility and forbearance as I worked on the book. Earlier versions of some sections have appeared in *CrossCurrents, Tikkun, CCAR Journal*, and the Australian anthology *Lifelong Learning and the Democratic Imagination* edited by Peter Willis and Pam Carden.

In a fit of isolation and despair I once thought of calling this book *The Emil Y. Nemo Lectures in Unsystematic Theology, Presented at the Niemandsuniversität Weissnichtwo* — an expedient which, thanks to my editors Jeffrey Robbins and Clayton Crockett, has not been necessary after all. For their immediate interest in the project and their intellectual adventurousness I am most grateful.

I suspect that friendship is my real religion — but friendship at an exacting level, liturgical both in its demand and in its transforming powers. A mutual integrity so rigorous, so generous and so tender changes the lights for us, in George Eliot's phrase; having experienced it, one cannot settle for less in the realm of religion. This book is for my two intellectual fixed stars: Sarah Thomson, who for thirty years has given my mind a place to work and to rest; and Joseph Boucher, who over the last nine years has become my conscience, and whose influence on this book I could not have predicted and cannot measure.

Chapter One

The Power to Contain

They do not accept their inheritance, and I inherit, not what
they inherited, but their abrogation of their inheritance.

—William S. Wilson, "Metier: Why I Don't Write Like
Franz Kafka"

The more [work] realizes and transforms itself in its object,
the closer it is to the imagination, to art, to culture; the more
it is unable to bring forth an object...the more it approaches
the condition of pain.

—Elaine Scarry, *The Body in Pain*

In criticizing recent liturgical language it is easy to appear merely
petulant. Liturgists, who are used to a certain range of negative responses — from inarticulate resentment to the passionate defense of
traditionalism for its own sake to accusations of heresy — are likely
to see any criticism as belonging to one of those categories. Even
an attempt to articulate clearly a sympathetic but critical stance is
bound to appear to some readers carping, small-minded, opposed to
creative experiment and to the reformers' own cultural critique. As
in national politics, a party that will not criticize itself assumes that
any critic is automatically an enemy, motivated by mere partisan
spite if not evil nature. But as in national politics, the situation is
more complex. A feminist may object to the simplistic representation of her feminism, even by her allies; a liberal Jew or Catholic
or Episcopalian may be demoralized not by the newness of the new

liturgical style but by its lightness; a heretic who takes her heresy seriously is likely to be annoyed at seeing it weakly presented. An outsider, knowing nothing of the history of liturgy but longing for some public expression of a profound private experience, may be dismayed at "welcoming" liturgies which overtly invite but covertly repel strong emotion. It is apparently hard for liturgical reformers to grasp that even their natural constituencies want to see the work done right: that the very people for whom the reforms are intended can be exasperated, even permanently disillusioned, by seeing their own ideas badly expressed.

In writing liturgy that responds to the contemporary sensibility but is less physically and emotionally persuasive than the work of the old guard, modern liturgists have not yet created a real alternative to the old forms. They have only created an agonizing split between the politically acceptable and the physically and emotionally satisfying. The standard response to complaints has been, for thirty or forty years, that justice is more important than aesthetics, that beauty will be along later, that over time we (or at least our children) will come to love the new inept language as much as we once loved the old polished words. But such a response presupposes that justice and aesthetics are separable, that justice incompetently applied can achieve its purpose. To offer politically contrived grammatical changes and carefully inoffensive metaphors to replace the language of brokenheartedness and ardor and fear is to understand very little about liturgy. In being willing to live with bad work for a generation or two, modern liturgists have abdicated — or have not even been conscious of — a responsibility. They assure us that the problems will solve themselves in twenty-five or fifty or a hundred years; they have not understood the social and moral debilitation entailed in living one's only lifetime with a liturgical language that cannot hold one's experience.

The premise of this book is the relationship between experience and speech: that we are compelled to speak our experience, and that there is a reciprocal relationship between the quality of our speech and our comprehension of our experience. The problem for modern liturgy is not, as it has usually been styled, the replacement of archaic diction with "accessible" modern language, or of oppressive patriarchy by egalitarian feminism, or any other paternalistic (or maternalistic) program for making religion safe. The real problem for modern liturgy — as for modernity in general — is how to survive modernity. It will not be solved by the imposition of a political schema on a religious one, or the undermining of a secular political order by a religious one, or by some specious "moderation" that tries to appease everyone and satisfies no one; so far as it is soluble, we will solve it by learning to speak once again as accurately as possible the language of brokenheartedness and ardor and fear. The very development of our language, its uses at moments of awe or moral reflection, its reemergence after great suffering — each of which I will consider in the following chapters — suggest that a profound language of prayer is *intrinsic*: that it is not too hard for us, neither is it far off, but already in our mouths and in our hearts.

It is a given that religious experience surpasses language. Yet the first thing we feel when we begin to speak of a religious experience is the imperative not to break faith with it. "What you want in poetry," says the poet Richard Wilbur, "is not rightness or wrongness of belief, but adequacy of attitude, a sufficient comprehensiveness and richness of attitude."[1] In a theologically driven religion the urge is always to fall back on rightness of belief, but attitude — the quality of our attention — is finally what makes a belief seem tenable. What the worshiper returns to in liturgy, both for its familiarity and for its disclosure of the unfamiliar, is a certain mental posture toward the unknowable — what St. John of the Cross called *un no sé qué / que se halla por ventura* (in Willis Barnstone's translation, "something I dont know / that one may come on randomly").[2] This recognition which is not definition, this disposition of the self toward something not the self, is returned to and returned to because it can be found nowhere else. There are no shortcuts through politics and sociology — or rather, liturgy that takes those shortcuts will produce people who take shortcuts with each other, who understand themselves and others merely as walking opinions or demographic types. Liturgy must overleap those categories, restoring the original *no sé qué* to everyone present, regardless of status or allegiance. The task may be impossible, but it is no less incumbent upon us; the inadequacy of language is, as it were, no excuse for inadequate language.

Liturgical language worth repeating functions on several levels. The body has something to satisfy it when the mind is estranged; the emotions have multiple points of contact; the intellect has absorbing occupation (always necessary to keep it from laughing). When these conditions are met, prayer unfolds in a trance of total absorption. This immersion in the experience accounts for the irrational rage of the worshiper when the trance is broken: the nagging self-importance of the updated pronoun or the tamed metaphor is an assault on one's deepest levels of concentration, an interruption and a crashing irrelevance, like a ringing phone during lovemaking. It is true that the old language, for a listener who has grown disgusted with it, will break the trance just as thoroughly; a friend leaving the Episcopal church at the height of second-wave feminism wrote a letter to her priest saying that every male pronoun in the liturgy offended her ear like a belch in the middle of an aria. But the same friend remains bereft of religion thirty years later, because she could find no adequate substitute for the rest of the language. In some sense that mattered, the new liturgies were all belch and no aria; they relieved an immediate need, but they were not song.

The language of the trance is not formulaic but holographic: any fraction reproduces the whole. After decades of inept revision it may be difficult for some readers to imagine how a mere phrase can bring trust and attention whole into the mind; what seems self-evident to a writer who thinks about rhythm and tone may not even register for some readers. But the old liturgies — for all their limitations — were largely a body of material that knew what introspection and moral urgency were, and how to help the worshiper to them. The new liturgies assume that introspection is no longer possible, and that moral urgency is satisfied by the revisions, and do everything in their power to distract the worshiper from them. Any fraction of their language remains a fraction: it can be tagged as either a survival or a correction of the old suspect forms. The revisions call attention to themselves with a kind of smug pride (*we* know enough to use this nonsexist locution, *we* know that calling God a king is benighted), and put the unrevised forms, which used to be merely normal — the backdrop for the worshiper's intentions, whatever they happened to be — in the position of calling attention to *them*selves with a kind of recalcitrant piety. Every form, every time, becomes at least partly a tug-of-war between traditionalists and revisionists, forcing every congregant artificially into taking one of these sides. Every phrase functions as a self-conscious statement of position and a demand for allegiance.

But the very thing liturgy is meant to reduce is self-consciousness. Even its introspection is meant to reorient the self, unsettling complacency and restoring a consciousness of the presence of God and the needs of the other. The self that knows what it thinks, and is chiefly set on making a public statement to the rest of the congregation, hears only its own voice.

The disruptive force of liturgical revision can only be justified if it establishes new habits of thought with a power equal to or greater than those being superseded. To introduce a new perspective in language incapable of sustained reflection is to erode one's own position from the start. Ian Robinson, deploring the revision of the Anglican liturgy, once said that "[i]n their extreme innocence about language these liturgists opted for a style in which their intention cannot be expressed."[3] Whatever the faults of the old language, it was at least not innocent; it knew its way around human nature, and it knew how to compel human nature by every trick and artifice of the senses to attend and to act. The new language thinks we only need to be told the right way to think, and that the liturgist's responsibility essentially ends there. Modern liturgy is (so far) a sketch, a caricature, not a fully developed form. It has been oppositional without having any fully realized place to oppose from; it has been geared toward making a counterculture, but not toward making a culture.

The attrition of religious belief that began with the Enlightenment was not the death of God but the death of a system of expression. From a language of the numinous that made no distinction between the literal and the metaphorical — the language of the medieval church, and of all unselfconsciously ardent religion in the mode that Owen Barfield calls "original participation"[4] — religious metaphor was progressively literalized in the centuries leading up to the Protestant Reformation. The church itself began the literalizing process, in the struggle to define and defend its doctrines; one had to believe, on penalty of death, that bread and wine really were transubstantiated to body and blood, that the dead would rise physically from their graves. Inevitably the literalism was taken further by the series of dissenters who could not accept the definitions. As the metaphors ceased to function on their own terms and became criteria of orthodoxy, religious language ceased to represent a relationship between the human and the numinous; it became a series of shibboleths for the enforcement of civil power by one group of people on another. Since for anyone who thought about them closely the metaphors patently remained metaphors, religious language became at the same time an outrage to the reason. What the Enlightenment did — what some intellectual movement sooner or later would have had to do — was denounce and dismiss the use of metaphor as a juridical tool.

But what the Enlightenment could not do was replace the spoiled metaphors. It replaced one literalism with another: the mortal disputes about the Real Presence with the intellectual razor's edge dividing fact from fancy. Religious metaphor was left intact — often it was treated with preternatural reverence — but it was put to one side while the real work of scientific discovery and technological development went on. Metaphorical language is, of course, ubiquitous, and remained indispensable in economic and political and scientific writing as in literature. But religious metaphor froze in the forms it had taken in the sixteenth and early seventeenth centuries, and some of the language of feeling froze along with it. These developments were originally and primarily Christian, but they influenced Jewish thought and liturgy in turn, as Jews were uneasily allowed into the intellectual life of Europe and attempted to create forms of prayer comprehensible to the surrounding culture.

It took two centuries — and the rise of anthropology and psychology — for "the numinous" as a category to be imaginable. For Rudolf Otto or anyone else to consider the *idea* of the holy, apart from its proprietary religious uses, marked a new phase in the study of religious experience (and perhaps in religious experience itself). Though Otto's primary attachment was to Christianity — in some passages to the point of chauvinism — his definition of the sense of the holy as an awe for the "wholly other" did more than salvage his own religion for a new generation of doubters. It took non-Christian religions seriously in their own right and reinforced the possibility of independent religious experience. Of course no religious experience is completely independent; there are always cultural particulars of imagery and practice in the background, and as Gershom Scholem once observed, a Christian mystic will not see Buddhist visions and a Buddhist will not see Jesus or Mary.[5] But the imagery of one's culture is a vehicle rather than a prerequisite; the experience can start from any point. In a culture without religious consensus, as ours has become, there will be unexpected collisions of imagery and radical alterations of practice. Even in a culture *with* religious consensus there are surprises: Dante's culture could have predicted Jesus and Mary in his imagery, but it could not have predicted Beatrice.

Independent religious experience is often disparaged as eccentric and undisciplined, but in another sense it is experience whose form is up to the numinous: it comes to the seeker direct in the seeker's own terms. Once uncanniness and unaccountability are factored in as attributes of the numinous, there is nothing to stop the numinous from showing up wherever it wants. Yeats's occultism, Matthew Arnold's melancholy unbelief, Dorothy Richardson's stream of consciousness, Proust's lingering attention to everyday detail are all visitations of the numinous without benefit of clergy, which arise from each person's particular combination of anxiety and receptiveness, need and desire. Twentieth-century liturgists, established in their own traditions, did not take much notice of this phenomenon, but Otto had understood it: "the numinous consciousness…cannot be 'taught', it must be 'awakened' from the spirit…[it] can only be induced, incited, and aroused."[6]

William James, writing roughly fifteen years before Otto, had prepared the ground by considering the essential likeness between nominally religious and nominally secular forms of conversion experience. So far had the religious and secular realms diverged by his time — and so similar are the forms of human desperation — that James could compare their common elements in neutral terms without a religious referent: the likeness between the sense of sin and the sense of shame (or profound inadequacy, or "irremediable impotence"[7]) that afflicts the soul in need; an intensification of this sense so intolerable as to bring the sufferer to a crisis; and the flooding in of a sense of salvation or "astonished happiness, and of being wrought upon by a higher control"[8] when the crisis is resolved. Otto's and James's categories — analytical in their detachment from particular dogmas and practices, but intimate in their knowledge of emotional life — make it possible to reconceive liturgy in forms that diverge from traditional theological categories. If, in James's terms, it is impossible to tell a subconscious influence from a supernatural one, deliverance is still deliverance.

James's method — which he both consciously derived from and ironically played off against scientific empiricism — was *subjectivity*: a serious critical attention to what people said of their own experience. As a psychologist in the early decades of psychology, James was among the first researchers to trust the subjective realm to illuminate otherwise inexplicable physical symptoms and behavioral patterns. In applying this method to the study of religion he established, in Kierkegaard's phrase, an "investigative rapport with actuality"[9] which could explore, rather than inevitably undermining, the sense of religious truth. But it was not only psychology that prepared the way for James's work. Subjectivity had also been the territory of those earlier spiritual freelancers, the Romantic poets — who trusted it so much, or were left with so little else to trust, that they began searching their own inner lives for revelation. If, within roughly two centuries, Milton's *Paradise Lost*, an epic of the fall of man, could be followed by Wordsworth's *Prelude*, an epic of the poet's own intellectual growth, something had happened to the holy: driven out of public life, or employed there only part-time as a figurehead, it sought refuge in the unchurched innards of the lyricists. Blake, Coleridge and Wordsworth — using essentially the same generalizing impulse that James and Otto would later use — found in Imagination the powers formerly ascribed to God. With the Romantics, "participation" began to return; for them the world was no longer mechanistic but charged with energy, even morally responsive. In Blake's "London,"

> the Chimney-sweeper's cry
> Every black'ning Church appalls;
> And the hapless Soldier's sigh
> Runs in blood down Palace walls.[10]

Wordsworth's boyhood terror after stealing a boat invested the very hills with the power of judgment, leaving him troubled by "a dim and undetermined sense / Of unknown modes of being."[11] The projection of moral awareness onto buildings and masses of rock — or, as the poets felt it, the *discovery* of moral awareness in them — differs from the Bible's projection of moral awareness onto God only in the degree of self-awareness that attends it: we do not have to argue over the historicity of Wordsworth's childhood emotions as we do over the revelation on Sinai. We accept a poet's report as a plausible account of his feelings, even when we take smoke and thunder at the giving of the law to be myth or special effects. "The pathetic fallacy," Ruskin called the ascription of feeling to natural objects, but he used the technique often and strikingly; fallacious or not, it is a mental move we make even when we know we are making a mental move.

In Barfield's anthroposophic philosophy, the evolution of consciousness entails the human race's eventual arrival at "final participation," which he describes as "the morality of imagination."[12] This is not a naïve return to the pre-rational but an awareness of ourselves as participants in the making of the world; it permits us to be ardent once again, but by a synthesis of ardor and reason, so that the lonely subjectivity transformed by deliverance can return to the community without forfeiting its own distinct consciousness. Barfield thinks the morality of imagination is what Jesus meant by "the kingdom of heaven is within you"; it may be what Jeremiah before him meant by the covenant written on the heart. It implies an internalized integrity, a code of action at once resolutely conscious and arising organically from the circumstances at hand, by which we can rise to the work of the numinous: not an inflated sense of ourselves as godlike or doing God's work, but a responsive attention to our surroundings and a matter-of-fact humility about cause and effect. The Romantics were only at the beginning of this shift of consciousness, searching most tentatively for its direction and often failing to find it, but they did show that in the absence of strong outer direction the soul will supply its own. Spiritual stasis — either in the form of settled religion or settled irreligion — is not, it appears, particularly stable; it will decay into unrest and begin the work over again.

Thus modernity tore down, but also renewed, the religious sense; by stepping outside the controversies of the Reformation and sidestepping the limits of Christian belief, it exposed the capacity for awe and moral seriousness as perennial and independent of dogma. Modernity as an intellectual movement has been unable to let religion alone; just as it took the religious works of Bach and Monteverdi and Machaut and Perotin from the ecclesiastical rubbish-heap and resurrected them in the concert hall, it has constantly probed the shape of God's absence through science and philosophy and literary studies. By desacralizing the world, modernity "murdered to dissect," but unexpectedly established — surely against its own will — that religion can be built again from the ground up. Protestant iconoclasm and Enlightenment rationalism have only brought us by another route to the essential Jewish insight: that the numinous is present and unconditioned, that it requires no representation, that it breaks into the world unexpected and even unwelcomed while refusing to be summoned on any terms but its own. Remove away every image of God, discredit every religious system as a spurious and corrupt human artifact, insist on the empirical method in everything, and the empirical method returns you implacably to the same religious conundrum: matter is spiritual. *M'lo khol ha-aretz k'vodo*, the whole earth is heavy with his weight.[13]

The instability of our subjectivity is bad for theology, which wants an Unmoved Mover. But it is the origin of liturgy. For liturgy, God is always a moving target: we pray to him and get equivocal answers, or none; we ask to see his glory and are shown only his back. Any assertion we make of God's grace and mercy is at once undercut by the contingency of our daily experience. Any assumption we make of God's indifference or hostility is eclipsed by the appearance of mercy and grace in our lives. The declaration from the burning bush, *ehyeh asher ehyeh*[14] ("I will be what I will be"), is a promise and a threat in equal measure, and hints at the simultaneous presence and absence of God at the other end of our prayers. Yet whether God is present or absent is not a final or even an answerable question, only a sort of spiritual brain-teaser by which our minds stay alert. With or without God, what is unequivocally present is the human other in need. The reality, and the alterity, of the stranger to whom we must do justice is so irreducible that even postmodernity, with its perpetually eroding certainties, finally arrives at it: the face of the other, and the voice of the other, and the vulnerability of the other. Levinas verifies what Blake knew at the outset of the return to subjectivity: *For Mercy hath a human heart, Pity a human face.* Erosion is our one certainty; from it all religion and ethics begin again.

But modern liturgy, which had every incentive to begin at this point, did not. Instead it moved, in Eric Caplan's excellent phrase, "from ideology to liturgy."[15] It passed its old formulas through the filter of Enlightenment literalism, purging them of ambiguity and religious anguish and reducing them to edification and reverie. With the loosening of traditional authority structures, liturgists apparently felt there could be no more commands: as though with a more democratic and less dogmatic emphasis a low standard of urgency was good enough, because religion could no longer seriously frighten us. In fact when institutional authority can no longer frighten us, the scope of our own responsibility can; there is greater need, not less, for moral and linguistic acuity. Edification and reverie are passive forms, which soothingly suggest that thinking the right thing is equivalent to doing the right thing. Instability and ambiguity, embedded in language of some permanence, are active forms that disturb and awaken us. The liturgists who tried to woo an ambivalent community back to the pews with relaxed standards of language and dress and self-scrutiny were on the wrong track: when people come back to religion it is responsibility that draws them.

Edification, in its original sense, has to do with building: raising the edifice of character, laying the foundations of moral personality. And if one can maintain a sense of character as *tabula rasa*, on which the accidents of genetic makeup and personal inclination and random experience can leave no mark, perhaps one can trust edification as a method. But accident is more potent than planned lessons; the stone the builders rejected has more impact than the builders would like to believe, and crazes the *tabula rasa* into splinters. Objectivity and detached analysis are deeply necessary for the sane conduct of life, but they are not sufficient. In Exodus 34 the broken tablets of the law, smashed by Moses in his rage at the golden calf, are replaced by another set; the first were written by God's hand and the second carved by Moses, and a minor undercurrent in Jewish thought surmises that the second set said something different than the first. Perhaps we replace the law given by God in fire and thunder with the law that we have seen with our own eyes, and in our own history, to be necessary — not out of slackness or arrogance, but out of more intimate knowledge. If there are no more commands, there are still imperatives.

Much of modern liturgical revision has been mere copy editing: removing *thee* and *thou* and their attendant verb forms (which are not difficult to teach, if anyone cared to), changing male pronouns to female ones or to passive constructions, using a flat word where a resonant or royal one is considered irrelevant, using an abstract noun where a metaphor is considered repellent. (The practice, when reading aloud from a prefeminist text, of extemporaneously substituting *God* for every male pronoun — "God will repent Godself concerning God's servants" — must be mentioned alongside this, as the practice most likely to inhibit the encounter with God; it will end as the stuff of parody and do women no favor.) Copy editing would appear to be a benign enough method, but it is seldom imaginative and can be applied with decided flatfootedness. The opening collect of the Anglican communion service was treated in this way. The old form — "Almighty God, unto whom all hearts are open, all desires known, and from whom no secrets are hid" — built both grammatically and emotionally toward a state of humility and receptiveness: "Cleanse the thoughts of our hearts by the inspiration of thy Holy Spirit, that we may perfectly love thee, and worthily magnify thy holy Name." In the revision it is only slightly altered: "Almighty God, to you all hearts are open, all desires known, and from you no secrets are hid: Cleanse the thoughts of our hearts by the inspiration of your Holy Spirit, that we may perfectly love you, and worthily magnify your holy Name."[16] The changes are few and simple — you can miss them if you read quickly with the eye — but to the voice and the ear they are fatally inane. The tension of the old version's subordinate clauses, which peel the heart like the layers of an onion, is flattened into a plain set of descriptors; God cleanses the thoughts of our hearts more or less automatically, because it's his job, not in response to our plea. The level of diction is inexplicably hybrid: it rejects *thy* and *unto* and *whom* but keeps the equally anachronistic *hid* and *that we may*. The effect — one suspects, the intention — is to short-circuit the established neural path from the words to the hearer's profound experience, while providing no compensating profundity. The old form keeps its eyes fixed gravely on God, while the new form has one eye nervously on the modern observer. The revisers no doubt thought that since the prayer still ended in "through Jesus Christ our Lord" it was still the same prayer; it *is* the same prayer, in the sense that a neutered cat is still the same cat. But the revisers had no sense of the violence that inept revision does to immensely delicate inward structures of response. If the neural path must be disrupted, disrupt it altogether and honestly by instituting a new one: *Almighty God, by whose design all things are mutable: steel us to suffer change, especially the loss of all that we most love; that we being tempered by dismay and stripped of possession, may trust in nothing but thine unmanifested goodness.*

But the revisers' concept of relevance is differently directed. It relies on the incorporation of current vocabulary and idiom as markers of up-to-dateness, rather than a felt sense of the congregation's complex experience in losing the old sensibility. Vernacular liturgy will always emerge when a population is steeped in a religious world view, and will always range from the sublime to the ridiculous, but the rhetoric of commercial popular culture clashes especially oddly with old liturgical speech patterns. Most people will be able to see the incongruity of the television jingle that enjoins Christians to

> Wor–ship the Lord and his Son,
> te–ll him that he's Number One![17]

But even more sober and literate efforts may shift rhetorical gears with disorienting speed. Lavon Bayler's metrical psalms borrow from politics —

> Suff'ring with us,
> Christ Jesus raises consciousness[18]

— and from business English:

> Your perfect love, O God,
> Revives our hearts and souls;
> Your precepts make the simple wise
> And redefine our goals[19]

— apparently with no sense of the oddity of the mix. Miriam Therese Winter's "Come, Spirit," which begins with a lovely simplicity, collapses with a clang and a giggle in the fourth line:

> Come, Spirit, as light in darkness,
> Come, Spirit, as rain in drought,
> Come, Spirit, as warmth in winter,
> Come, Spirit, and bail us out.[20]

Both Bayler and Winter are highly literate in their traditions and show thorough competence with rhythm and diction aside from these incautious rhymes, but there are things one should not do for a rhyme; a breath of carelessness will damage the mood. The worshiper, whose feelings have been softened and coaxed forth only to be disappointed, responds, *No, they didn't mean it, they didn't get it, what do they take us for?*

At a more sophisticated theological level, old formulas and prayers are recast in interpretive form. The practice has honorable precedent and considerable potential, but it exposes the interpreter's imaginative and tonal range to pitiless comparison with the original. Perhaps the point of highest intensity in the Jewish liturgical year is the *Unetaneh tokef* prayer at Rosh Hashanah and Yom Kippur, which presents human fragility at its most extreme:

> On Rosh Hashanah it is written and on Yom Kippur it is sealed: how many shall die and how many shall be born, who shall live and who shall die, who shall die in his time and who untimely; who by fire and who by water, who by sword and who by wild beast, who by hunger and who by thirst, who by earthquake and who by plague, who by strangling and who by stoning; who shall rest and who shall wander, who be at peace and who tormented, who shall be poor and who rich, who shall be brought low and who exalted. But repentance, prayer and deeds of justice can temper the force of the decree.[21]

A supplementary responsive reading in the Conservative movement's prayer book works hard to make the prayer edifying rather than terrifying:

> When we really begin a new year it is decided,
> And when we actually repent it is determined:
> *Who shall be truly alive and who shall merely exist;*

Who shall be happy and who shall be miserable;
  Who shall attain fulfillment in his days
  And who shall not attain fulfillment in his days;
Who shall be tormented by the fire of ambition
And who shall be overcome by the waters of failure;
  Who shall be pierced by the sharp sword of envy
  And who shall be torn by the wild beast of resentment;
Who shall hunger for companionship
And who shall thirst for approval;
  Who shall be shattered by the earthquake of social change
  And who shall be plagued by the pressures of conformity;
Who shall be strangled by insecurity
And who shall be stoned into submission;
  Who shall be content with his lot
  And who shall wander in search of satisfaction;
Who shall be serene and who distraught;
  Who shall be at ease and who shall be afflicted with anxiety;
Who shall be poor in his own eyes
And who shall be rich in tranquillity;
  Who shall be brought low with futility
  And who shall be exalted through achievement.
But repentance, prayer and good deeds
have the power to change the character of our lives.
  Let us resolve to repent, to pray and to do good deeds
  so that we may begin a truly new year.[22]

No doubt there is something to be said for not encouraging people to believe in a real heavenly book in which God writes our deeds and which he seals on the Day of Atonement. But there is nothing to be said for the softening of the essential point that we do not know the hour or manner of our death. By recasting each kind of death as a metaphor of personal growth, the prayer replaces the horror of contingency with the self-absorption of neurosis — as if fire and water had ceased to be lethal, as if hunger and thirst were obsolete, as if there were no plague worse than the pressures of conformity.

The old prayer's stark confrontation with time is deflected into the leisured emotional lint-picking of the affluent. How could any rabbi writing after the Second World War have thought starvation and displacement and sudden death might have no relevance for a congregation of Jews?

The small and recent movement called Reconstructionist Judaism, which in some ways is well placed to make liturgical experiments — being strongly committed both to preserving an extensive Hebrew liturgy and to interpreting Judaism for the modern condition — may be taken as a microcosm of the general liturgical trend. The movement's founder, Mordecai Kaplan, was a rationalist who deplored biblical literalism; largely to shore up the credibility of Judaism for his own skeptical immigrant generation, he conceived it not as a religion in the limited sense but as an evolving civilization.[23] In his prayer books he preserved much of the traditional God-language out of a general acceptance of the necessity for metaphor, but his deletions — Jewish chosenness, the resurrection of the dead, and the personal messiah — were points he did not consider metaphorical or negotiable. Not only for Kaplan, but for the conference of orthodox rabbis who denounced and burned his 1945 prayer book, these were matters of literal belief or unbelief. Not all liturgists, especially in Christian circles, are so frankly rationalist, but most liberal liturgists find supernatural language an embarrassment, and the desire to avoid embarrassment casts a certain guardedness over all their expressions of feeling. An intellectual honesty based wholly on rational assent does not allow the free development of aesthetic honesty; instead it creates an unexpected alliance between the rational and the sentimental. In Kaplan's interpretive reading based on the morning service's traditional blessing for light, cosmic pageantry is recast into an idealized picture of our response to a God we can postulate somewhere behind "nature." The traditional prayer is full of biblical imagery: "All exalt you, creator of all, who opens each day the doors of the gates of the east, who brings forth the sun from its place and the moon from its dwelling place, and who lights the world and those who dwell on it, which you created with [your] quality of mercy." Kaplan's version goes:

> With the dawn, nature's familiar shapes and colors emerge from the darkness to delight us afresh with their variety and beauty. And with our awakening from slumber, our senses and our spirits respond anew to the splendor of Thy world....Grant, O God, that our gratitude for all the beauty, order and power that reveal Thee in nature impel us to serve Thee. May nothing that we do mar the holiness of life by causing any fellow creature to lose the joy of living.[24]

Kaplan's prose is easy to read, and the Hebrew is at a disadvantage in having to be translated, but in the long run "familiar shapes and colors," "delight us afresh" and "respond anew" actually work against the awakening of the senses; they provide reassurance that everything is happening on schedule and there is no need for acute attention. (Note that nature's familiar shapes and colors have no definite shape or color, unlike the sun and the moon; where the original prayer is understated but specific, Kaplan's version is lyrical and vague.) The delight is faintly perfunctory, as if reason is not powerful enough to ignite the emotions and must borrow used ones. Where the old prayer preserves a remote and hieratic sense of the heavens going about their business whether or not we have the wit to be awed by them, Kaplan's interpretive prayer is only a step away from Ecclesiastes' jaded "there is nothing new under the sun." The perfunctory mood is a minor current in long-enduring liturgies generally; a typical instance is an 1874 Anglican communion hymn by William Bright which begins "And now, O Father, mindful of the love...,"[25] as if the parishioners are all rising creakily from their knees with the same sense, just short of tedium, that this has all happened thousands of times before. Kaplan's "impel" is good, but "beauty, order and power" are only half the evidence of God in nature; one is inclined to think of tooth and claw, flying branches in storms, ice under car wheels, disease vectors, "order" that is disorder to its victim. The claim that we can avoid "causing any fellow creature to lose the joy of living" — as parents, as citizens, as omnivorous mammals — seems to call for a complete overhaul of the educational system, radical prison reform, and the enforcement of international law, and even then an apologetic footnote would be needed to explain that one's breakfast does not lose the *joy* of life if it has lived happily to the end. Mark Twain had a better grasp of reality with his satirical prayer admitting that we are not equally delighted with *all* creatures great and small:

> O Source of Truth, we have lied, and we repent. Hear us confess that which we have felt from the beginning of time, but have weakly tried to conceal from Thee: humbly we praise and glorify many of Thy works, and are grateful for their presence in our earth, Thy footstool, but not all of them.[26]

It is not unreasonable to ask that liturgists think their thoughts through to the end; the congregants certainly will.

Kaplan's inheritors have been critical of the affective thinness of his work;[27] they have sensed that even if supernatural language cannot be taken literally, it powerfully assists emotional response. The 1994 *Kol Haneshamah* Reconstructionist prayer book reintroduces angels, kabbalistic liturgical poems, and mystical names of God; it has erudite footnotes on the ancient meanings and modern relevance of the prayers and calligraphed pages in the style of medieval amulets. Its intellectual content is often impressive, deeply informed in the tradition and searching intelligently for ways to apply the old texts to current thought and conditions. Unhappily, its emotional content is aggressively inane; interspersed among the erudite footnotes are numerous free-verse effusions that could have seen print in no other context, and the translations not only recast but often launder the old texts. Readers whose Hebrew is weak can get no sense of the literal meaning of the words; the editors seem at some points actively to want to conceal the meaning, an unfortunate impression in an egalitarian movement. The translator, Joel Rosenberg — whose "wondrous poet's ear" is celebrated in the preface[28] — takes a bold and sometimes interesting approach, but with uneven judgment: "Teach [these words] *intently* to your children"[29] is a striking reworking of what is often rendered "diligently," and "Refine our hearts to serve you honestly"[30] is a fine modern rendering of a phrase sometimes translated "Purify our hearts to serve you in truth," but "Your power and support are there to comfort me"[31] reduces Psalm 23's "Thy rod and thy staff they comfort me" to flat psychobabble. In Psalm 90, "You return a person unto dust" is a hash of modern casual and old elevated idiom which clearly wishes only to avoid the word *man* at any cost, and "Oh, let us know how to assess our days" is no improvement on "Teach us to number our days." "Give us, at daybreak, the plenty of your love," is a graceful and ardent elaboration of the Hebrew,[32] but "Regale us for as many days as you have tortured us" sets a frivolous verb against a painful one to the benefit of neither.[33]

One of the book's most awkward experiments is the revival of an old Sephardic custom of replacing God's unpronounceable Name with a series of honorifics. In Sephardic custom this seems an intriguing way to handle the proscription of God's name, but the Reconstructionist editors take it as an opportunity to invent new ungendered titles and experimental metaphors. In Rosenberg's translation this results in lines like

Listen children, hear me out,
an awe for THE MYSTERIOUS I'll teach to you.[34]

and

> I rejoiced whenever people said to me,
> let's journey to the house of THE UNSEEN![35]

— this latter a mixture of the demotic, the formal and the programmatic so weirdly incongruous that one listener has reacted with a stilted Bobbsey Twins enthusiasm — "Yes, let's do!" — and another with a teen-movie scenario: "Yeah, let's see how many we can fit in the car! You bring the six-pack!" One can have every sympathy with the impulse not to say "God" or "the Lord" at every turn, and yet think some of this is risible even on the first reading.

It is inaccurate to call such passages aberrations or insignificant lapses; they are published work meant for regular use, written according to conscious policy and not rejected at the editorial stage. Reconstructionists are conscious enough to leave good records of their intentions; it is clear that they do mean this language as a better alternative to the old forms. Richard Hirsh, taking a more Kaplanian stance than Rosenberg's, remarks on the paradox of retaining traditional supernatural language while giving it an essentially naturalistic reading; he regrets the dearth of frankly non-theistic paraphrase in *Kol Haneshamah*, to "send a clear message" of the movement's theological position. Like Kaplan, he is not hostile to metaphor, but also much like Kaplan his idea of "non-personal, reflective poetry" sidesteps metaphor entirely and replaces it with abstraction. "It should not be the responsibility of the simple, nor the burden of the sophisticated," he protests, "to process intellectually the conversation theology of the prayer book so that 'Blessed are You, Guardian, Israel's redeeming power' comes out something like 'In moments of redemption, we become witnesses to and partners in the work of freedom.'"[36] Of course not; it happens faster and more intuitively than that, in a rush of gratitude rather than a ponderous detour. The Greek meaning of the word *metaphor*, "to carry across," suggests a sort of instantaneous bridging of the gap between the right brain and the left; it is not a kind of circumlocution, but the shortest distance between two points. The human mind has all sorts of tricks of consciousness besides rationality, one of which is to address a projected part of the self or the universe as *you*, and both the "simple" and the sophisticated take it as seriously as they need to on any given occasion.

If Kaplan's rationalism was directed toward a skeptical generation whose parents had fled the pogroms, his successors' strategies often seem aimed at the skeptics' grandchildren who would not object to being Jewish if they could square the theology with casual rationalism or with Buddhist and New Age practice. David Teutsch, editor of *Kol Haneshamah* and now president of the Reconstructionist Rabbinical College, says that he and his committee were concerned to provide "a theology that we can comfortably affirm."[37] One need not think of God as anything more than a character in a book to notice that God does not seem to have intended Jewish existence to be comfortable. A more orthodox position would not automatically confer more theological stamina; Orthodox Judaism codifies Jewish discomfort through a rigorous ritual practice and a stringent apartness from the wider culture, but Orthodox prayer book commentaries are as liable to complacency and edification as liberal ones. Jewish liturgy has, in a sense, been going down this road for a long time; it started as soon as the rabbis bowdlerized Isaiah's *I make peace and create evil* to the prayer book's *Who makes peace and creates all*.[38] Rabbinic Judaism in general, influenced as it was in a roundabout and generally unacknowledged way by Greek thought, absorbed Plato's suspicion of the poets. But the Hebrew Bible makes no clear demarcation between poetic and moral thought.

Theologians, naturally enough, think liturgical language expresses a theological stance. It does more; it is the concentrated essence of the relationship between the self of the worshiper and the self of the universe, which is imagined as a personality that knows us more intimately than any human personality, even our own. Like any other profound relationship it is full of intuitive leaps, protestations of gratitude, puns, recollections, long-term ironies, regrets and resentments; it will not fail us and it will not spare us. The more complete and absorbing the relationship, the less intelligible it will be to someone who does not share it, yet it is not always true that anyone not in on the game will be confused or bored witless by it; some will be instantly drawn to it. Certainly anyone who takes full part in the relationship will not be satisfied — indeed, will feel agonizingly thwarted and chaperoned — by approximations and substitutes.

Clergy and liturgists do face a dilemma when they try to reformulate traditional prayers: the conflicting needs of religious insiders and religious outsiders, people who have felt trapped in a religion they cannot believe in and people who have felt shut out from a religion they cannot have. Both groups may want something other than the traditional formulas, but in the short run they may want different things. The cool rationalizations that can keep the first group in the pews may be a welcome alternative to barbarous talk of the blood of he-goats and bullocks, or the Blood of the Lamb; whereas rationalizations may hold no appeal for the second group, whose own blood is suffused with some insistent hormone of religious longing which abstractions will not appease. Someone who has been wrenched out of secularity, or out of a former religion, by exigent spiritual need may have no patience with euphemism. Yet when the needs of the outsider are fully addressed, those born to the religion may find themselves similarly moved; there are not so many differences between outsiders and insiders that a powerful phrase cannot bridge them. Any religious service may serve as the entry point for a person who needs transformation; any private anguish may open a habitual congregant's eyes to words read a hundred times before. These are the people whose intellect and energy can transform religion; it matters, every time, to give them something worth longing for.

Both insiders and outsiders may be particular about theological content — not surprising, when theology is so often presented as the real point of liturgy — and some may prefer credible content in unmemorable style to untrustworthy content in memorable style. But others will feel, usually without being able to articulate the feeling, that unmemorable style *is* untrustworthy: if you cannot say what you have to say in words that command attention, it may not be worth saying at all. It is not easy to convey this feeling intelligibly to liturgists who work in the ideological mode. A nuance shrinks away and hides from a political program; it is impossible to advance the shy claims of the body against the confident assertions of the wave of the future. Yet the body's claims do not go away, while the one thing certain about the wave of the future is that it will sometime break and withdraw. Liturgists whose sole consistent criterion for acceptable language is that it not offend the current sensibility have no means of calling the current sensibility to account, and no resources for surviving its demise. Teutsch says frankly of one liturgical decision, "I have no illusion that this formulation is eternal, no certainty that it will survive even thirty years. *But it says what we felt it ought to say.*"[39] One ought to be taking thought for the next thirty years; in the sense that eternity is not simply infinite time but infinite truth, one ought to be taking thought for eternity. The liturgical statement we can "comfortably affirm" is not only expedient but disposable. It may be comforting, and to that extent palliative — for the next thirty years, or the next thirty seconds; in the long run it has no coherent aim. "Today" — *ha-yom* — is always decisive in biblical thought ("choose this day whom you will serve"), but not in the sense of eclipsing the past and the future.

In one of the few articles devoted to the aesthetics of modern liturgy, Michael Signer laments that high-powered achievers feel infantilized by the "poetic and figural language" of old liturgies, and postulates that this is because such language is not efficient and does not tell them what to think:

> In order to comprehend their sense of deprivation at worship, we should contrast the prayer book with a text that many worshipers read more frequently, the *Wall Street Journal*....A quick scan...allows for a maximum comprehension of the current state of affairs, worldwide. From the center columns, the eyes move laterally to take in pithy accounts of complex issues in business and politics. The language of the articles is concise and concrete. The numerical and statistical format of much of the information leaves little opportunity for vagueness or uncertainty. By the time you complete a reading of the *Journal* you have a clear sense of the world and the direction your own affairs should take. The connection between life and the marketplace is immediate and obvious.... [In a typical Reform Jewish liturgy] [i]t is never entirely clear whether the entire congregation comprehends the service of the day.[40]

The Reform service presents particular problems in giving only a fragmentary outline of a much denser service, and a heavily interpretive translation of such Hebrew as remains; it has made a great many decisions beforehand about how much the congregation can handle. The level of Reform prose style is often impressively high even in the interpretive translations (thanks largely to the work of Lawrence Hoffman), and taken as a whole does present a serious confrontation with Jewish history and moral imperatives; but it is difficult to take as a whole, both because of its interrupted movement and because of the many new English readings that function more or less at the level of the Hallmark card. A meditation preceding the Mourner's Kaddish, for example, offers "Praise for the presence of loved ones...the ennobling aspirations...the precious moorings of faith," and for "the God of our people, the Source of all growth and goodness, the Promise on which we build tomorrow."[41] The recent enthusiasm in some quarters of the Reform movement for the full Hebrew liturgy suggests that the congregation is ready for harder work. High-powered achievers can handle complexity if they are offered complexity; if they feel a sense of deprivation at worship it may be from being presented with a language they do not know and are not given the tools to learn, together with new prayers that are clearly counterfeits and decoys.

More promisingly than his initial argument would suggest, Signer eventually proposes Aquinas's aesthetic as a basis for liturgical discourse: *Ad pulchritudinem tria requiruntur: integritas, consonantia, claritas.* He gives Stephen Dedalus's idiomatic translation from Joyce's *Portrait of the Artist as a Young Man*: "Three things are needed for beauty: wholeness, harmony and radiance." But he immediately retracts the suggestion, adding self-deprecatingly that the paradigm "might be a bit too ambitious for liturgical studies at present."[42] So it might well. Prayer book committees tend to be small groups of colleagues who have to go on working together; they are charged with preserving a body of work for which many of them have only a qualified enthusiasm. Who will tell a colleague that a new bit of writing is bad, subliterary, unfit to stand next to Isaiah or Deuteronomy or the Psalms? A prayer book invites the reader to rise to the level of its writers, and no higher; if it is not aiming at Isaiah or Deuteronomy or the Psalms it is aiming too low. Whether or not Signer's paradigm is too ambitious — or *because* it is too ambitious — it is in fact the one thing imperative for liturgical studies at present. Imagine liturgy animated by such ambitions: integrity, consonance, clarity.

The idea of liturgy as literary language may be jarring. One is almost abashed, in the present climate, to propose it; it seems gratuitously cruel to set the productions of most modern liturgists beside verse and prose, which after all they were not trying to equal, their definition of "creativity" having evolved along other lines. But literature is by definition made of language worth listening to.

Literary scholarship, which has no formal commitment to religious belief or practice, has no trouble with the idea that religious language is naturally difficult:

> [L]ogical integrity is rarely the goal of authentic God-talk, but is in fact its peril, for a language which reduces God to the convenience of human reason surrenders religious wonder to a demeaning literalism....Like all serious God-talk, [George Herbert's "A Parodie"] strives with whatever means it can to wrench, bully or cajole a generally uncooperative, earth-bound language structure into evoking awarenesses its grammar was originally designed to filter out.[43]

The difficulty is intrinsic to any language that approaches the unsolved problem, the unmet need and the inexpressible perception. Religious language is intended, in a sense, to return us to a time before grammar: to a time when our language had to be constructed from hints and guesses in an environment overloaded with meaning, when we were seeing and saying everything for the first time. Syntax fractures under the strain. Liturgy is not the medium of the "quick scan," but of the stammer, the repetition, the child's phrase practiced over and over. It accurately reflects religious experience in being almost too vivid and particular, but with gaps; its difficulty comes from the alternation of preternatural brightness with an absence of orienting signs. "Something I dont know / that one may come on randomly." Literary language has been willing to approach such states even as religion has tried to retreat from them.

Literary language is essentially *authoritative* language. It is not always elevated or elaborate but is just as likely to be blunt. Fiction and poetry detonate in us the depth-charge of recognition; we read them for the pleasure of the words in our mouths and the explosions of truth in our minds. If we read liturgy expecting no such pleasure, and only such truth as may have passed the scrutiny (or escaped the attention) of the prayer book committee, we are aware at some level that it fails. Liturgy in its origins is a communal, democratic and tuitionless point of access to strong feeling and moral reflection; it must be held to the same standard as any other writing we would willingly read over and over. It serves less the function of a settled catechism and more the function of a public library, which admits all comers. (Public libraries do a roaring trade in genre fiction, of course, but good genre fiction surpasses contemporary liturgy in vocabulary, in narrative vigor, and in competently approaching a task; one could do worse than emulate it. Even an opiate needs the right molecular structure.)

Religion itself is, in an important sense, a branch of imaginative literature — an invented world, or a world in the act of being invented, which by nature demands of us a certain suspension of disbelief. Though literature is not canonical in the biblical sense (perhaps no longer even in the academic), it is the direct inheritor of the Bible in Western culture; its moral concerns and even some of its narrative strategies bear the indelible biblical stamp. The boundaries between religion and literature have been at times highly permeable; in English the galvanic influence of Reformation piety on the development of secular literary forms, and later the Romantics' substitution of subjectivity for religion, are obvious instances. If the Bible makes no structural distinction between revelation and literature, neither do the novelists and poets who inherit it. Both the Bible and the novel insist that we shall not avert our eyes: we do not learn our way around moral life by remaining innocent of the immoral, or by merely denouncing it. Knowledge of good and evil is the biblical method, indispensable since Eden; liturgy cannot discard it.

Biblical and liturgical quotation quickly became a standard part of the secular repertoire; there are so many points of contact that literary quotation might conceivably become a standard aspect of liturgy. There is the question of intellectual property — nine-tenths of powerful liturgy is plagiarism, a practice no longer permissible in an age of copyright law and citations — but a phrase does not thoroughly belong to a culture until it is widely quoted. Liturgical use disseminates words that are felt to be crucial knowledge. The relationship between literature and liturgy has been opaque to modern liturgists, who sometimes believe in literary inclusions but treat them roughly like dance numbers in musical comedy, suspending prayer while a poem or prose passage is read in its entirety. As a rule the selections are made with extreme caution for "accessibility" and not for the crucial nature of the words; a remarkable exception appears in Jules Harlow's (Conservative) Yom Kippur liturgy, a section from Anthony Hecht's poem "The Hard Hours" in which is embedded a line of Shakespeare — Lear's "none does offend, none, I say, none,"[44] an extraordinary association for the Day of Atonement and as accessible as anything you will ever read. But Shakespeare's line might have been even more striking buried somewhere in a paragraph. Literature as interruption is unfair both to literature and to prayer, and not many whole poems will stand up to such use. Certainly it is better to have one line of Shakespeare embedded in a passage of fast-moving language than fifty-six lines of Marge Piercy that bring the action to a standstill.

Franz Rosenzweig thought it a mistake to distinguish the "religious" from the "aesthetic" aspects of a religious text at all, as though form and content were separable in this of all realms:

> An aesthetic object striving to be art for art's sake, a poetry altogether free of prose are of course notions that can arise only in opposition to the wildly extreme notion of a "purely religious" object, an absolutely unpoetical prose. (Moreover: if on the aesthetic side there arises the sin of being only for oneself, then on the religious side the ghastly mirror-image of that sin can arise and be embodied in response.) But where the aesthetic object does not become an absolute, neither does the religious object; it does not reduce itself to a special, religious subset of culture, but remains in possession of all its connections with reality — aesthetic

reality included. Religious discourse does not then sink into the prose of bare "content"; rather it must — for it cannot do otherwise — avail itself of all means of expression, must sound all tones, must possess all its apparently fixed and prefabricated, independently transmittable "content" only by grace of the transient moment of oral expression.[45]

That is to say, religion for religion's sake is as solipsistic a form of tail-chasing as art for art's sake ever could be — a little ingrown world of seminarians with their guitars and their favorite tunes, their comforting exegeses of disquieting texts and their artless verses, all of which convey a strong whiff of the dorm room. Rosenzweig is, of course, alluding to Hillel's conundrum: "If I am not for myself, who will be for me? And if I am only for myself, what am I? And if not now, when?"[46] If art for art's sake is the equivalent of being only for oneself, then the "ghastly mirror-image," being *not* for oneself, is religion for religion's sake at its most patronizing: the shepherd who knows just what the sheep need to hear, the liturgist who writes to instruct and console while his own vulnerabilities remain untouched and his own subjectivity unfed. Religion is for grownups, and for children who are not enjoying being young; a liturgist who does not aspire to the one state and remember the other will not succeed.

There is a crucial difference between "authoritative" and "authoritarian," which politicized ears may miss. The authority of literary language is temporary and not meant to compel obedience; what it compels is attention, and a long-incubating response which cannot be predicted or tracked. Old liturgies were always a mix of the authoritative and the authoritarian; more recent ones, unable to master the authoritative, have become authoritarian against their own principles. Indeed, perhaps it is because they cannot imagine an authority they can respect that they cannot quite become an authority the reader can respect, but must resort to extraliterary insistence. Feminist liturgy starts from a general assumption that traditional liturgy is essentially propaganda, consciously aimed at the maintenance of patriarchal privilege and the exclusion of women; since propaganda is taken to be the defining element of liturgy, "gender-sensitive" liturgies tend to feel like nothing so much as propaganda, imposed by (no doubt unintended) authoritarian fiat of the most unchallengeable kind. Yet, at a level unknown to writers of propaganda, intelligence creates intelligence and dignity creates dignity, whatever the pronouns; morally acute language creates morally acute listeners, and not by moral exhortation but by the instantaneous grasp of a truth that is moral, physical, emotional and intellectual at once. People speak of compelling language; they mean precisely language that renounces compulsion.

Elitism is the automatic accusation against literary language — "Simple people love this stuff!", I was once told by a minister — but the charge is misplaced. It is not "elitist" to offer skilled work to people who might not otherwise have access to it, even if they might not instantly understand it; it is "elitist" to *withhold* it from them on the grounds that they could not possibly understand it. People with graduate degrees and secure positions — people who associate intellectual work with credentials and material rewards, rather than a craving for knowledge beyond their reach — are always intervening on behalf of the disadvantaged to deny them access to seriously expressed thought and feeling; they say "that's too difficult for the uneducated" when what they mean is "I don't want to be made to work that hard." In fact it is not fundamentally a question of education or class; the "simple," if that is the right name for people who love this stuff, are as likely to come from the suburbs as from the city or the country, and from the professions as from the trades. It is not a question of economic but of emotional crippling, and *emotional crippling can be relieved*; we know it in therapeutic terms and should know it in liturgical terms. There are two pressing reasons to develop profound and demanding new liturgy: because it offers intelligence and splendor impartially to everyone who participates in it, even if

plendor nowhere else in their lives; and
ught, intermittently — perhaps no more
else — to acts of conscience, and liturgy
em there. Even if we take the overriding
solation, what could be more consoling
te can be brought to acts of conscience,
our mouths?

he Soviet Union and its satellite states
an integrity made absolute under pressure, longing
for freedom of speech as the medicine of their condition — knew the
uses of authoritative language. Their poems were circulated underground, memorized and recited; the writers were vulnerable to every
kind of surveillance and punishment because their words had an
audience. After the collapse of the Soviet Union, some immigrants
to the West discovered that people *with* freedom of speech are beset
by another, perhaps more debilitating, condition: the disbelief in the
integrity of words, the despair of finding freedom through speech.
Americans, as a rule, do not memorize and recite verse; our minds
fill up, more or less unconsciously, with advertising jingles and the
lyrics of popular songs. Our strange mix of material well-being and
emotional poverty puzzles us; we do not look for trustworthy meaning in words, beyond what we can call "meaningful." If Adorno's
pronouncement that there could be no poetry after Auschwitz has
thus come true in this backhanded way — not through renunciation
but through confusion and hesitation — it has been through this
half-conscious sense of democracy as a kind of permanent permission to aspire to less. An East German refugee to the West just after
the fall of the Berlin Wall observed: "You can say anything here, and
nobody listens to you."[47]

It may be the business of the Western liturgist to feel that vacuity as pressure: to search insistently for language that must be
listened to, language that cannot function as propaganda, language

independent of politics or at least in sufficient tension with politics to be unpredictable. Liturgy makes nothing happen, as Auden said of poetry; the slow elaboration of wordplay takes too long, both to write and to live with, and one cannot trace its effects. Yet in another sense it makes everything happen. The literary writer may shun performative speech — Auden, it is said, was asked to rewrite the Book of Common Prayer and refused — but censors and dictators know: the writer's influence is performative, every time. Perhaps liturgy of this kind is the most profound and secret underground writing we can conceive. We may think of it as the Western *samizdat*, circulated in the most extreme obscurity among writers and readers who would not last a week on a prayer book committee: tentative, not even sure of its audience, no threat to either political or religious authority because both consider all liturgy so utterly negligible.

"I like a look of agony," said Emily Dickinson — no churchgoer — "because I know it's true."[48] A look of agony is the last thing a modern prayer book will allow. Its business is theodicy: papering over the cracks, whitewashing the bloodstains, conducting damage control on God. Religious insiders, who have heard every variety of theological spin, and religious outsiders, who come to ritual under inner compulsion and often in great trepidation, have already seen the truth beneath the whitewash: God *is* damage. If God is also solace and regeneration, we will not arrive at that knowledge by being assured of it constantly in words that do not bear repetition. Only a fundamental reordering of our perceptions will serve: that "brief struggle for capacity" of which Dickinson spoke elsewhere, which occurs when the mind encounters something too large for it. "The power to contain," she said,

> Is always as the contents
> But give a Giant room
> And you will lodge a Giant
> And not a smaller man.[49]

Chapter Two

The Synaptic Gospels: Speculations on Liturgy and Cognition

Unless you are at home in metaphor, unless you have had your proper education in the metaphor, you are not safe anywhere. Because you are not at ease with figurative values: you don't know the metaphor in its strength and in its weakness. You don't know how far you may expect to ride it and when it may break down with you. You are not safe in science; you are not safe in history.

—Robert Frost

One needs infinitely distant sentences that one barely understands, as a mainstay over the millennia.

—Elias Canetti

If the idea of liturgy as a literary form is suspect, we might do worse than begin with linguistics. Humans are speaking creatures; we are not quite satisfied that we have experienced our experience until we have passed it through language. Even in a field whose experimental methods are fairly hard-nosed and objective, linkages between language, emotion and moral reasoning are found; objectivity, when it is diligently objective, discovers that subjectivity does not go away. There are limits to the usefulness of defending art through science, but if our response to language can be seen as a feature of our cognition and not simply an anomaly, we may at least have established that "bare content" is insufficient for public prayer.

The Mouths of Babes

The investigation begins humbly, with Jean Piaget and Lev Vygotsky listening to the babble of children. What Piaget termed "egocentric speech," and later researchers including Lawrence Kohlberg have sometimes called "private speech"— young children's way of talking to themselves as they play, of chanting their thoughts and actions aloud — seems to be an essential phase in the early development of language. A preschool child will prattle away in apparent disregard for whether anyone is listening; she makes no effort even to make sense to a listener, not from any deliberate secretiveness but from a casual disregard, even unawareness, of any difference between her own outlook and the hearer's. Piaget calls private speech in the presence of a hearer "collective monologue"[1] — which is to say that it is not dialogue; it is speech practicing itself without any particular need for a response. Kohlberg, Yaeger and Hjertholm characterize it as "a running stream of commentary upon the self's activity to an auditor who is neither clearly the self nor clearly the other."[2]

Piaget and Vygotsky differed on the nature and function of private speech. Piaget, noting that the habit gradually disappears in the early school years, concluded that it was presocial: that speech without intent to communicate simply atrophies at around the age of six or seven and is replaced by social speech, as the child has the first confused glimmerings of cause and effect and the first intimations that not all points of view are mutually intelligible. On the whole, Piaget meant "egocentric" in a descriptive and not a pejorative sense; nonetheless Vygotsky finds a streak of disapproval in Piaget's picture of the oblivious three-year-old, just out of the "autistic" stage of the pleasure principle and incapable of reason, who has no particular wish to be understood and who must be inducted into the realities of responsible social discourse.[3] Piaget's implication seems to be that private speech is aimless and in a sense developmentally useless, nothing more than a marker of immaturity. Vygotsky thought all speech was essentially social from the moment the child asks for milk, that the child does not resist but desires linguistic development. For Vygotsky private speech is *para*social, a movement toward communication:

> Three-year-olds do not have a logical outlook, and this absence of a logical attitude is incorrectly taken as a sign of the child's egocentrism. Three- to five-year-olds while playing together often speak only to themselves. What looks like a conversation turns out to be a collective monologue. But even such a monologue, being the most spectacular example of child "egocentrism," actually reveals the social engagement of the child's psyche. A collective monologue does not require either a purposive isolation or autism. Children who are participants of the collective monologue do believe that they communicate with each other. They believe that their thoughts, even those that are poorly expressed or unarticulated, belong to all participants.[4]

Vygotsky's experiments were structured so as to test the social aspect of private speech. He showed that private speech increases in the presence of an obstacle: more intellectually challenging forms of play bring it out. The preschool child, not yet capable of conceptual thought, works from "a certain deficit of conscious control"[5]; speaking aloud is a means of bringing the obstacle to consciousness in order to establish control. Thus one of the primary functions of private speech is self-guidance or problem-solving. "It does not merely accompany the child's activity; it serves mental orientation, conscious understanding; it helps in overcoming difficulties; it is speech for oneself, intimately and usefully connected with the child's thinking."[6] The presence of (potentially) comprehending observers is critical: private speech increases in the presence of others, especially of other young children, and drops almost to nothing if the others are deaf or speak a foreign language.[7]

Far from atrophying and being replaced by social speech at school age, according to Vygotsky's theory private speech is gradually internalized into the half-verbal shorthand of unvoiced thought. It does not disappear, but becomes more completely private. Vygotsky notes the increasing obscurity and complexity of private speech as the child's vocabulary and range of interests develop; rather than becoming more comprehensible to a hearer, it becomes less so. Cognitively speaking, Vygotsky believes this to be the convergence point of intellectual and linguistic development; before it, speech has been essentially preintellectual and thought prelinguistic, and after it "thought becomes verbal, and speech rational."[8] Egocentric speech is "speech on its way inward"[9]; it is "a phenomenon of the transition from interpsychic to intrapsychic functioning, i.e., from the social, collective activity of the child to his more individualized activity."[10]

Instead of the "spread of affect" or "affective contagion"[11] that is the only communication possible in the absence of language, thought is "a dynamic system of meaning in which the affective and the intellectual unite."[12] We can think about feeling — and think *by means of* feeling, and feel by means of thought — at a complexity far beyond either pure rationality or raw emotion. Wordsworth's exact and delicate phrase "feeling intellect"[13] carries no scientific weight, but it conveys instantly (and without the need for experimental proof) the quality of responsive attention that the fusion of thought and feeling allows.

Clearly, private speech has no precise adult equivalent; adults think, and then engage in dialogue or write books. On the other hand, the phenomenon of prayer, seen through the lens of Vygotsky's research, looks curiously like an adult, codified version of the child's spontaneous talk. Addressed as it is to a hearer who is hypothetical and never replies — and whose reply is not really expected, or not in words — and motivated as it is by the taxing moral dilemmas of physical and spiritual life, prayer meets the basic criteria for private speech. It is meant for overhearing; it is a form of self-guidance or problem-solving; and it increases in the presence of an obstacle. When spoken in a community of human overhearers — or read in solitude from the community's book, which maintains the community's presence even in its absence — prayer becomes "collective monologue" in a complex sense: the individual reads her own needs and circumstances into the words of the prayers, but knows that everyone else in the community does the same with *their* needs and circumstances, so that there is an overlap between one's own perspective and another's. The "auditor who is neither clearly the self nor clearly the other" may be understood by turns as the community and God: the neutral, essentially sympathetic presence of the congregation encourages the speaking aloud of self-guidance, and the imagined presence of God sustains in the speaker a more profound sense of being heard. Inasmuch as the prayer book maintains the community's presence even in its absence, it suggests God's presence even in *his* absence: both solitary and communal worship become charged with a sense of mutual attention, even when physical mutuality with a bodiless God (or for Christians, a resurrected and ascended God whose body is sacramentally identified with the Word but consumed as mute matter) is impossible.

Prayer may, of course, be extemporaneous, and in that sense is like private speech in its spontaneity, though it still follows familiar coded patterns of theology and phrasing. But formal written liturgy functions as the private speech of a whole culture. Like the maturing child's increasingly idiosyncratic private speech, it is incomprehensible to anyone outside its context: Vygotsky is very clear that the shift from private speech to the adult mixture of inner speech and verbal thought is a shift from biology to culture,[14] and liturgy may be a prototypical example. For those who share its context, prayer is a direct line to a culturally mediated expression of experiences with some resemblance to one's own; for those who do not, the context must be learned. Because it is culturally mediated it is not neutral — it is intended to shape one's thinking — but over time it can also bend to accommodate one's thinking; as with culture in general, the influence is reciprocal.

Writing, as Vygotsky points out, is a much later development in a child's life than speech, and a more laborious one. It is a third level in linguistic functioning: beyond spontaneous private speech and "condensed, abbreviated" inner speech, writing entails "deliberate semantics — deliberate structuring of the web of meaning."[15] It is a far more conscious proposition, with specialized rules of intelligibility. Nonetheless writing presupposes and depends on the writer's having passed through the earlier stages; some of its most valuable turns of phrase and organization arise from unconscious forces, and the most compelling writing never quite leaves oral language behind.

Kohlberg, Yaeger and Hjertholm[16] were curious whether private speech is more closely linked with isolation or sociability in children: is it more used by the less cooperative, less socially expert children or by the popular children? Slightly more often (among younger children in particular) they found it was used by the popular children, supporting Vygotsky's contention that private speech is parasocial rather than Piaget's belief that it is presocial. Liturgy, perhaps, is more ambiguous; it may be simultaneously a way-station toward social interaction for misfits (and thus parasocial) and toward inwardness for the gregarious (and thus, so to call it, paraspiritual). But it does serve as a meeting ground for "all sorts and conditions of men,"[17] and thus to a greater or lesser degree relieves isolation.

The problem-solving intent of prayer operates at various levels of complexity. Sometimes it is very direct, as in this Maori invocation before hunting:

> Mother Earth,
> I am coming down to step on your back.
> I am holding the bow.

I am holding the arrows.
I am going to kill a pig.
My name is Mai Kivavia.
I am standing under the Ipi tree.
I am going to kill a pig.[18]

The hunter speaks his actions, declares his preparedness and his intention, locates himself by name and in space for the (imagined) ear of Mother Earth on whose (metaphorical) back he is standing. Yet already something more is going on here than solitary problem-solving: the focusing of intention and the insistent repetition point to a quasi-hypnotic readying of the self to undertake an act requiring muscle, quick reflexes and courage. The intimate and essentially benign relationship between the speaker and Mother Earth is assumed; the need for powerful initiative on the part of the speaker must be asserted.

On a somewhat less direct level a prayer may locate the speaker in time and space without setting a specific problem, in order to establish a more general readiness. In the Hebrew *siddur* (here represented in translation), the section of the morning service called *birkhot ha-shaḥar* or morning blessings assembles the self piece by piece upon waking — a work of construction requiring daily repetition:

Blessed are you, Lord our God, king of the universe, who
   gave the rooster understanding to distinguish between
   day and night.
Blessed are you, Lord our God, king of the universe, who
   did not make me a gentile.
Blessed are you, Lord our God, king of the universe, who
   did not make me a slave.
Blessed are you, Lord our God, king of the universe,
   [*men*:] who did not make me a woman.
   [*women*:] who made me according to his will.

[Liberal prayer books, uneasy with the previous three blessings, phrase them in the positive: who made me a Jew; who made me free; [*men and women*:] who made me in his image.]

> Blessed are you, Lord our God, king of the universe, who gives sight to the blind.
> Blessed are you, Lord our God, king of the universe, who clothes the naked.
> Blessed are you, Lord our God, king of the universe, who releases the bound.
> Blessed are you, Lord our God, king of the universe, who straightens the bent.
> Blessed are you, Lord our God, king of the universe, who spreads the earth on the waters.
> Blessed are you, Lord our God, king of the universe, who has provided for all my needs.
> Blessed are you, Lord our God, king of the universe, who firms man's footsteps.
> Blessed are you, Lord our God, king of the universe, who girds Israel with strength.
> Blessed are you, Lord our God, king of the universe, who crowns Israel with glory.
> Blessed are you, Lord our God, king of the universe, who gives strength to the weary.[19]

The progression from inward to outward and from the domestic to the social and planetary is a daily reminder that God is the maker both of one's simplest bodily functions and of the whole world. Another morning blessing praises God for the functioning of the body's many ducts and cavities, and is traditionally recited after using the bathroom.

Vygotsky notes a shift in private speech from simple running commentary to commentary that includes an element of planning.[20] This distinction is observable in prayer as well. Some ostensibly petitionary prayer can be more accurately seen as a form of self-conditioning, or resolution: the *siddur's* "Guard my tongue from evil and my lips from speaking guile"[21] and Psalm 19's "May the words of my mouth and the meditations of my heart be acceptable in thy sight," are not so much requests for help as reminders to the self to govern its speech. Psalm 137's "If I forget thee, Jerusalem, let my tongue cleave to the roof of my mouth" is a more desperate form of self-guidance, a fierce effort to keep faith with what has been lost. Even the New Testament's "Give us this day our daily bread"[22] may have more to do with the means of production than the lilies of the field; to cast oneself on God's mercy is to cast off anxiety, and to have more energy for the task of making a living. Petitionary prayer is a way of handling an obstacle — over which one has, like the pre-conceptual three-year-old, "a certain deficit of conscious control"; it may be a way of gaining that control through taking charge of the situation, or relinquishing control by learning to endure it.

Jewish prayer includes some deliberately private undertones to public moments: variants recited by the congregation when the cantor is singing something slightly different, and in at least one case a radically different undertone to a particularly mysterious occasion. During the threefold blessing of the *kohanim* or hereditary priests on Yom Kippur — "The Lord bless you and keep you; the Lord make his face to shine upon you and be gracious to you; the Lord lift up his face upon you and give you peace"[23] — the congregation, forbidden to look at the *kohanim*, is given this to recite:

> Master of the universe! I am yours and my dreams are yours. I have dreamed a dream and I do not know what it means. May it be your will, Adonai my God and God of my fathers, that all my dreams, of myself and of all Israel, be for goodness — those I have dreamed about myself, and those I have dreamed about others, and those others have dreamed about me. If they are good, strengthen and bolster them, and may they be fulfilled in me and in them, like the dreams of Joseph the righteous. But if they need curing,

cure them like Hezekiah king of Judah from his sickness, and like Miriam the prophetess from her leprosy, and like Naaman from his leprosy; and like the waters of Marah by the hand of Moses our teacher, and like the waters of Jericho by the hand of Elijah. And as you changed the curse of Balaam the wicked from a curse to a blessing, so may you change all my dreams, of myself and of all Israel, for goodness. And keep me, and be gracious to me, and accept me, amen.[24]

The prayer only appears in Orthodox prayer books — liberal Jewish editors in a post-Freudian age have naturally found it incomprehensible — but apparently it arose in the Babylonian exile, when sufferers from nightmare would bring their distress to the priests.[25] It has fallen out of favor now as a distraction from the mighty and resonant priestly blessing, but it was not necessarily an error; it was an attempt by both dreamers and liturgists to grasp something inchoate, open-ended and impossible to take hold of by ordinary means. The terrors of the mind are a challenge to established religious custom; the simplicity of "I have dreamed a dream and do not know what it means" — something that might happen to anyone — is a tremor at the foundation of the whole elaborate superstructure of priesthood and sacrifice. The cult, and its exilic survival in the persons of the *kohanim*, must be able not only to discharge its duties as prescribed in the Torah but to respond to the unconscious human neural quirks of sleep. The prayer's catalogue of biblical cures acts as a restorative to the consciousness shaken by nightmare; the annual, scheduled recitation of the prayer before the *kohanim* asserts the claim of disruption on the formal schema of blessing. As in Kafka's parable of the leopards, whose marauding in the temple becomes so predictable that it is scheduled into the ritual, contingency and custom can come to terms.

For the really insoluble problem, death, the strongest liturgical responses are so striking in their bravado as to uphold the mourner by the sheer density of their improbability. The Christian assertion of glory after death in spite of the evidence is made forcefully in Paul's extraordinary passage, often read at funeral services:

> It is sown in corruption; it is raised in incorruption: it is sown in dishonor; it is raised in glory: it is sown in weakness; it is raised in power: it is sown a natural body; it is raised a spiritual body....Behold, I show you a mystery; we shall not all sleep, but we shall all be changed, in a moment, in the twinkling of an eye, at the last trump: for the trumpet shall sound, and the dead shall be raised incorruptible, and we shall be changed. For this corruptible must put on incorruption, and this mortal must put on immortality.[26]

In Judaism, the Mourners' Kaddish recited at the end of every service makes no mention of death; it is an intense and accumulative praise of God whose function was originally (as it still is elsewhere in the service) simply to mark the end of a section. Eventually it began to be used to mark the end of a scholar's life, and then of anyone's life; gradually it acquired purgatorial meanings, which Leon Wieseltier's *Kaddish* investigates in their full oddity. The modern skeptic, for whom praying one's parents or lover or child out of purgatory is a ludicrous and repellent notion, has access to a more naked and terrible meaning: when the deficit of conscious control is complete, there is nothing left to do but praise God. We are to affirm that the world is filled with God's glory when it is empty of the one we have lost. The outraged consciousness recites the prayer numbed or weeping or raging; meanwhile the very verb forms (*yitbarakh, yishtabah, yitpa'ar, yitromam, yitnasei*) rock the unconscious tenderly and bring it relief.

One of Vygotsky's most pregnant hints is his distinction between a word's "sense" and its "meaning": the meaning is the simple denotation, and the sense is "the sum of all the psychological events aroused in a person's consciousness by the word."[27] A major impetus behind recent liturgical reforms, as in Reconstructionism, has been the question of meaning, the call for liturgy to say what it means and mean what it says. Yet even the great compliment of the imperfectly articulate congregant, "That was such a *meaningful* service," edges away from the implication "It was meaningful because I knew what it meant" and toward the intimation that psychological events have been stirred. A simple and literal understanding of "meaning" leaves no room for the sense — for all the associations that come with the word, which may go well beyond any doctrinal assertion or commonly accepted belief. In the new liturgical landscape, the intent seems to be to arouse at most one psychological event in the consciousness.

Ritual, of course, is sometimes said to be marked by an entire absence of meaning — and not only by rationalists for whom "meaningless ritual" is as automatic a phrase as "machine washable" or "standard transmission." Frits Staal's influential essay "The Meaninglessness of Ritual" contends that ritual is entirely "self-contained and self-absorbed"[28]: rather than being a set of acts with symbolic meanings, it is a set of acts that cannot be decoded, which are strictly carried out not for what they mean but purely for their own sake. Ritual is gratuitous, intrinsic, without practical results in the world: "pure activity, without meaning or goal."[29] Staal asserts this not only of ritual acts but of ritual speech: the genuinely meaningless syllables included in some Vedic rituals exemplify "syntactic structure in its pure form, hence pure activity"[30] — perhaps like children's nonsense syllables or adult glossolalia, and in some respects like liturgical Greek, Latin, Church Slavonic or Hebrew for worshipers who do not fully understand them. (*Kyrie eleison, misericordia tua, Gospodi pomilui, shema kolenu*: if these phrases stir psychological events, it is partly through their departure from the vernacular and their association with ritual, though each is understood at a general level to be a plea.) Though the effect is different for expert readers of the liturgical language, the ritual association still adds an element of something not *less than* but *more than* meaning.

The techniques of group recitation contribute to the sense of ritual as "pure activity": the beehive hum of Jewish *davvenen*, in which everyone chants softly aloud at a different pace; the ethereal unison of Gregorian chant; the subdued spoken unison of Anglican prayer. The very intonation of liturgical prose differs from other speech in its absence of affect, even when the words are laden with affect; the linguist David Crystal observes that in unison prayer read from a text there is very little variation in tone:

> Any participant in a congregation may, if he wishes, articulate his words with as much feeling as possible, introducing a wide range of pitch patterns; but as far as the total, cumulative auditory effect is concerned, such effort is unnecessary, and few speakers bother. A congregation...has very much one voice....The pitch level on the whole is low and monotone, though towards the end of a longer stretch of utterance than normal there may be a noticeable descending movement. This is absolutely predictable at the very end of a prayer, where the 'Amen' (and often the words immediately preceding it) is given a marked drop in pitch. But otherwise pitch contrasts are regularly reduced to zero, leaving monotone and rhythmicality as the defining characteristics of unison liturgical prayer.[31]

Individual prayer, whether read from a text or spoken extemporaneously, follows the same pattern, and has one other striking feature:

> [T]his is one of the few cases where one is allowed to speak with little or no significant kinesic accompaniment: we find a minimum of facial expression and bodily gesture in this modality, a marked contrast with sermons.[32]

"Allowed" suggests that the liturgical monotone is a relief: from social obligations, from the need to respond to the other or to get one's meaning across, from every kind of scrutiny except that of one's own conscience. It is thus more on the side of the paraspiritual than the parasocial. But rather than conveying a *lack* of meaning — particularly among "peoples of the book," for whom the language of ritual does have a marked intellectual content — the monotone liturgical recitative indicates a tension or interplay between meaninglessness and meaning. The recitation in an emotionless tone of the strongly emotive language of prayer may indicate either rote inattention *or* highly compressed and deeply reserved emotion; the monotone is a safeguard that makes it impossible for an observer to tell which is which. Yet the presence of the observer is a necessity, and the sense of the observer's understanding and essential sympathy a precondition, for the emergence of the speech. Like an old couple eating dinner in a restaurant without speaking, a congregation need not always be smiling and chatting to be present to each other — or to God.

Staal, noting the complex embedding of smaller units of ritual within larger ones and the modification of these units for particular occasions (as the Catholic and Anglican masses always include a collect for the day, and the Jewish *Amidah* includes certain blessings on weekdays, others on the Sabbath, and special additions for new moons and festivals), was struck by the similarity of his diagrams of the rules of ritual to linguists' diagrams of the rules of syntax. He goes so far as to claim that syntax *originates* in ritual[33] — that the cognitive paths of sentence structure, and the inexplicable linguistic division between sound and meaning (which Vygotsky alludes to in his discussion of the separate development of thought and speech and the revelatory discovery that things have names[34]), were established in prehistoric and prelinguistic ritual practice. Given the peculiarities of a genetic structure built up not by logic but by accretion, with many meanderings and repetitions, such an idea may be far-fetched, but is not impossible. Established patterns do function as templates for new ones. Certainly our neurological structure adapts and compensates for many kinds of injury by recreating a lost pattern in a new place; it may have given rise to ritual and syntax either successively or simultaneously. As far as our ability actually to establish what happened in prehistoric and prelinguistic times, syntax and ritual may bear the same relation to each other as the chicken and the egg; what is clear is that both our cultural productions and our perception of those productions are patterned.

Kohlberg, Yaeger and Hjertholm note that "[the] parasocial confusion of self-guidance and communication makes the self-guiding function of egocentric speech both uneconomical and inefficient."[35] Self-guidance in general is inefficient — the self sometimes complies, sometimes resists — and prayer, as an apparently gratuitous and generally repetitive action, is entirely uneconomical. But most of our means of learning through creature-comfort are uneconomical — meandering, cyclical, impossible to organize or standardize. There is a general tendency toward waste in nature: all those apple blossoms that never become apples, all those sperm that die on the way to the egg, all those bad drafts to make one good one. We make more than enough so that some of it may be enough. Liturgy, with its needless repetitions and layers of meaning, follows the pattern; as a form it is intrinsically inefficient, even overdetermined. It fits Lewis Hyde's category of "gift labor," which includes all work too essential to be paid (the work of intimate relations like motherhood, sexual love and friendship), or to be adequately paid (teaching, social work, ministry, the arts). How many times is "enough" for a mother to hug her child? for lovers to kiss? for friends, or teacher and student, or therapist and patient, to talk? How many times is "enough" to say the morning blessings? To quantify such a thing is to misunderstand it. The ambling movement of discovery not driven by a goal — spiritual indirection, one might call it[36] — is the only route to the intense moments of focus in which intention, repetition and revelation converge. Virginia Woolf says somewhere that marriage is a succession of days during which nothing much happens, till after so many days a "bead of sensation" is formed; without the opportunity created by uneventfulness, there could be no event.

The Mind and its Maps

As a lay person investigating a new, highly complex and open-ended field, one is likely to get waylaid in cognitive science: to get caught up in fascinating specifics like Steven Pinker's mention in *Words and Rules*[37] of the role of front and back vowels across many families of languages. The pattern is always *pitter-patter, dribs and drabs, this and that, here and there*, with the front vowel preceding the back vowel — never *patter-pitter, that and this*; it provides a way to test the satisfaction quotient of a new phrase. For the critic of liturgy there is suddenly a physical explanation, beyond any theological or political stance, for why the traditional Jewish blessing formula *elohenu melekh ha-olam* (our God, king of the universe) is more satisfying than one current alternative, *elohenu hei ha-olamim*[38] (our God, life of the worlds): it speaks better. For the feminist anti-monarchist the alternative is certainly preferable, and *hei ha-olamim* has been used elsewhere in the tradition; but *elohenu melekh ha-olam* moves from front to back in the mouth, whereas the vowels of *elohenu hei ha-olamim* stay stammeringly at the front. The consonants of *melekh ha-olam* work fluidly together, whereas the syllables *henu hei ha* demand quick work at the back of the throat. Pinker's observation that higher front vowels are generally used for what involves the self, and lower back vowels for what involves the other[39] might further imply — for the really disagreeably obsessed liturgical critic — that *elohenu hei ha-olamim* does not set up a mutual relation between self and other but subliminally insists *hey, hey, me*. As a replacement for a constant and central formula — *melekh ha-olam* is in perpetual use in Jewish prayer, recurring far more often than *through Jesus Christ our Lord* in Christian liturgy — it is consequently not a good bet.

Writers, and not only literary writers, do work by such principles; comedy is heavily dependent on them, and writers who want to avoid unintentional comedy may find it useful to know them. Phyllis Diller is said to have honed her comedy routines on the principle that the joke-word must come last and end in an explosive consonant. The strategic deployment of vowels is an essential part of comedy: what would *H.M.S. Pinafore* be without the short *i*, as the chorus declares that in spite of our hero's humble birth he *is* an Englishman, spinning the vowel out (staccato, in some performances) into *For he is an I-i-I-i-I-i-I-i-Inglishman!* The popular singing trio The Roches has built a whole style of poignant and intelligent comedy on the American accent at its least refined, repudiating all singing-master's advice about rounded Italian vowels and holding diphthongs like *oi* in *That's not the point* and syllables like *er* in *As far as I'm concerned* (in precisely calibrated harmonies) for several counts.[40] These principles operate whether or not they are consciously applied; liturgical writers ignore them at their peril, especially when they hope to supplant forbears who were highly trained in oral rhetoric.

But cognitive science illuminates far more for the liturgist than the feel of a phrase in the mouth. Its descriptions of mental activity fit so closely the patterns of ordinary thought and linguistic behavior as to seem intuitively accurate. A comprehensive and interlinked picture emerges of linguistic, aesthetic, intellectual and moral activity. After centuries of bad guesses and Procrustean efforts to make the brain fit the theory — from the onerous demands of pure reason to imaginative caprices like the Oedipus complex to the artificiality of artificial intelligence — a description like psychiatrist John J. Ratey's is strangely recognizable:

> The brain...does not process information and construct images by manipulating strings of digits such as ones and

zeros. Instead, the brain is largely composed of maps, arrays of neurons that apparently represent entire objects of perception or cognition, or at least entire sensory or cognitive qualities of those objects, such as color, texture, credibility, or speed. Most cognitive functions involve the interaction of maps from many different part[s] of the brain at once.... The brain assembles perceptions by the simultaneous interaction of whole concepts, whole images. Rather than using the predicative logic of a microchip, the brain is an analog processor, meaning, essentially, that it works by analogy and metaphor. It relates whole concepts to one another and looks for similarities, differences, or relationships between them. It does not assemble thoughts and feelings from bits of data.[41]

Recognition of similarities — between objects, people, musical phrases, ideas or situations — does, in everyday experience, come whole. The resemblance between the teacher and Donald Duck is instantaneous and cannot be unthought once perceived; the echo of "Itsy-Bitsy Spider" in the tune of the prayer colors one's sense of the words; the metaphor or the pun settles instantly into its place, and the laugh or the groan follows.

Since metaphor is such a contentious crisis point in theology and liturgy at present, it is hopeful to find it occupying such a fundamental position in our neurological makeup. Theologians have only recently become willing to admit that God-language is metaphorical, but they have been earnestly at work ever since on adjusting the metaphors. Some of these adjustments, predicated as they are on acceptability, suffer from an almost physical deficit that makes them incapable of inspiring ardor or igniting the associative powers. One cannot imagine a metaphor conceived in such earnestness as the germ of any artist's best work; most efforts recall Bowdler and Polonius more than Bach or Rembrandt or Donne. If metaphor involves the whole brain and not just the consciousness, the generation of metaphor must allow access to the whole brain rather than shutting off certain corridors.

In research preceding the rise of cognitive science, metaphor was already being described as something more oblique than a one-to-one symbol system — as something more like "sense" than "meaning" in its breadth and adaptability. Donald Davidson offers the striking (and metaphorical) definition of metaphor as "the dreamwork of language."[42] Metaphor tells the truth but tells it slant; its aim is not simply to compare an unfamiliar thing with a familiar one, but also to establish familiarity between speaker and listener. Ted Cohen, in an essay on "Metaphor and the Cultivation of Intimacy," sees the offering and reception of metaphor as involving three reciprocal steps: "(1) the speaker issues a kind of concealed invitation; (2) the hearer expends a special effort to accept the invitation; and (3) this transaction constitutes the acknowledgment of a community."[43] The aim of metaphor is as much social as descriptive, a sort of dance of approach and mutual consent.

Cohen adds that the process is not always benign; there is the possibility of hostile metaphor — intimacy established with intent to shame, and advanced without mutual consent:

> Intimacy sounds like a good thing, and I have been urging attention to the use of metaphor in its cultivation. It is not, however, an invariably friendly thing, nor is it intended to be. Sometimes one draws near another in order to deal a penetrating thrust....Some of the most instructive examples will be ones in which intimacy is sought as a means to a lethal and one-sided effect.[44]

The biblical prophets used a good deal of hostile metaphor in their unremitting effort to convince Israel of its corruption; their sexual metaphors are among those that most horrify feminist commentators, together with the biblical metaphors for God like father, king, and warrior that once established intimacy and are now felt as hostile. But even a genuinely repellent metaphor, embedded in a historical text, is something more complicated than an assault on the modern self. It is also — it is *therefore* — a direct line to the numinous: the very shock of it unsettles one's categories and stirs up difficult questions. A deliberately innocuous counter-image is not so much a genuine invitation as a warning or a territorial marking; it tells you what questions to ask by having already answered them. Congregants can tell an edifying metaphor a mile off, by the scent of stagnation, and may prefer a hostile metaphor if only for its brute vitality.

Metaphor that strikes feeling into response, rather than rendering it unnecessary, achieves the union of intellect and affect that Vygotsky identified as intrinsic to thought. Paul Ricoeur suggests that metaphor is intimately bound up with the "structure of feeling": it is not a purely intellectual move, but an instantaneous and profound response to a situation. Feeling has both spontaneity and deliberation; it is quick in its arrival, but it arrives so quickly because thought has prepared its way. Feeling arises, perhaps, when the brain sees a relationship — when metaphor springs up between two disparate phenomena that are suddenly related by a thought. For Ricoeur, feeling is "a process of interiorization":

> To *feel*, in the emotional sense of the word, is to make *ours* what has been put at a distance by thought in its objectifying phase. Feelings, therefore, have a very complex kind of intentionality. They are not merely inner states but interiorized thoughts. It is as such that they accompany and complete the work of imagination as schematizing a synthetic operation: they make the schematized thought ours....[The function of feeling] is to abolish the distance between knower and known without canceling the cognitive structure of thought and the intentional distance which it implies. Feeling is not contrary to thought. It is thought made ours.[45]

Thus what happens when we respond to a formula like "Blessed are you, Adonai, redeemer of Israel" is not — as Richard Hirsh assumes — "intellectual processing"; it is emotional ingestion. We make such a formula "ours" not by abstract paraphrase but by attaching it to our own experiences of deliverance. We become willing to address a personal God not by fudging the definitions till we come up with one we can tolerate, but by momentarily needing so badly to thank *something* that we have to say "you." Belief, assent, is the wrong paradigm; it is what the kabbalists called *d'veikut*, cleaving.

Through this emotional attachment to a thought we begin to build a network, a scaffolding, of deeply felt understandings — part image, part idea — that can be trusted. Otto recognized that this process was cumulative: "It is a well-known and fundamental psychological law that ideas 'attract' one another, and that one will excite another and call it into consciousness, if it resembles it. An entirely similar law holds good with regard to feelings."[46] (Elias Canetti puts the matter more feelingly: "One sees thoughts stretching their hands out of the water, one believes they are calling for help. A mistake: They live below, intimate and very familiar with one another, just try and pull a single one out alone!"[47]) Otto emphasizes the permanence of these attractions, when we feel them as fundamental: "The 'association of ideas' does not simply cause the idea *y* to reappear in consciousness with the given idea *x* occasionally only, it also sets up under certain circumstances lasting combinations and connexions between the two."[48] Functional liturgy establishes these connections for a whole community and across generations — not through an idea we can "comfortably affirm," but through an idea that widely and consistently provokes feeling.

Metaphor and Morals

Israel Scheffler, writing at a point when cognition was still understood primarily as reasoning, made an effort to establish the idea of cognitive emotions, two of which he identified as "the *joy of verification* and the *feeling of surprise*."[49] Subsequent research has linked cognition and emotion more thoroughly, and located certain neural relationships between them; Scheffler's rather specialized identification of emotions *about* cognition ("something is verified that I thought was so"; "something happens that I had not anticipated") has become part of a wider picture of the mutual influences of perception, emotion and thought.

Similarly, it may be worth speculating on the idea of *moral* emotion — a concept that would have been at home in the nineteenth century, with its preoccupation with duty and self-regulation, but is not out of place in the twenty-first with its interest in the neural roots of our common behavior. What cognition and morality have to do with each other has not been thoroughly explored, and there might be debate over what a moral emotion is; fundamentalist religion makes much of repugnance as a moral emotion, and defends it (for example, in the case of homosexuality or abortion) with reasoning about the nature of the human body or the good of society or simply as an innate reaction not needing defense, whereas liberal religion feels repugnance toward other objects — war, the death penalty, environmental pollution, fundamentalist religion — and tends to justify the repugnance by the effects of the phenomena. Perhaps the most that can be said is that repugnance is a hard-wired capacity that can be trained in one or another direction; it can be a moral emotion but can also be indulged to excess or passed down as a prejudice, whereupon it is no longer quite operating in the moral realm. Similarly, duty can be understood as a transcendent calling or a crushing imposition; something depends on the preparedness of the person whose duty it is, though it cannot be predictably said that an unprepared person can avoid, or will fail in, the duty. Immediately the moral legitimacy of the emotion becomes bound up with the situation: one has to know the details.

Linguist Mark Johnson, in an imperfect but suggestive sketch of the cognitive roots of morality, has proposed that moral decisions themselves operate by analogy and association rather than by predicative logic and detached analysis. As we would expect by following a line from Otto to Vygotsky to Ricoeur (or perhaps the line would have to begin with Wordsworth), Johnson finds that in moral thinking "[t]here is no separation of intellectual precepts from feeling and imagination."[50] We do not make decisions in cold blood but from a desire to live out an intelligible pattern.

Johnson is struck by the distinction between what a philosopher means by a rule and what a linguist means by a rule. For a philosopher a rule is prescriptive, and arises from a strenuous and conscious process (like *Thou shalt not commit adultery*); because it is conscious it must perpetually be reinforced in the consciousness to keep it from atrophy. For a linguist a rule is descriptive; it denotes a non-conscious and effortless process, and is self-reinforcing because hard-wired (like the functioning of front and back vowels as Pinker describes it — or like the actual incidence of adultery in American society as Kinsey described it, though in this case it is really the impulse and not the activity that may to an extent be hard-wired). Johnson believes that our moral reasoning is based not so much on the first kind of rule as on the second: not so much on general precepts obediently followed as on "cognitive prototypes" imaginatively applied (like our observations of other people's marital devastations and our reading of novels, which may do more than precepts to warn us against rash experiment). When a set of precepts actually functions as a cognitive prototype — a possibility Johnson does not mention — it is not exclusively on its own merits but by association with people and communities who have made the precepts seem workable and desirable. There is more to good morality than "good morals"; in the unforeseeable situations that break into our lives and require our best judgment, we make our decisions so as to reproduce patterns that the people we honor have reproduced. A moral precept may be so far abstracted from any definite context as to be impossible to apply to one's own; the truths of fiction, poetry and in some cases even gossip may be more helpful. From this point of view the business of liturgy is not so much to instill the precepts as to draw the maps by which moral need can be understood.

Liturgists who work in the edifying mode are essentially on the side of the philosophers: moral precepts must be introduced preemptively, reinforced frequently, and imposed as a template on our experiences and our decisions. Liturgists who work in the associative mode, so to call it, would be on the side of the linguists: moral precepts make themselves felt acutely in need, enforce themselves more swiftly and accurately than the concepts of reward and punishment can quite keep up with, and fit themselves with exquisite accuracy — and often with exquisite pain — to the shape of the situation. In this view, liturgy is not so much a work of instruction as a work of integration; not so much a court of law as a mobile emergency unit equipped for stark actualities.

For Johnson, moral reasoning is a process of transforming disconnected and random events into the sense of a purposive life, through the cognitive work of metaphor and narrative:

> the synthetic unity supplied by cognitive models, metaphors, frames, and narratives [is] the overarching ordering that transforms mere sequences of atomic events into significant human actions and projects that have meaning and moral import. Every one of us is actively plotting our lives, both consciously and unconsciously, by attempting to construct ourselves as significant characters within what we regard as meaningful life stories.[51]

A narrative includes an *agon* that must be resolved; decisions emerge through the synthesis of sequential events into life stories.[52] Johnson's schema is neither free-willed to the point of "creating one's own reality," in the New Age phrase, nor entirely deterministic; he sees us as having body and imagination within a constrained freedom. We are drafted into our situation in life, and have a problem set for us by virtue of our time and place and family. Our problem is only roughly similar to anyone else's; universal moral rules can address the similarities but cannot make sense of the differences. We are not usually faced with a sharply discernible contrast between good and evil alternatives but with a tension between incompatible goods. In making a decision we are seldom telling Satan to get behind us, but rather are sacrificing one possible good outcome in favor of another. The fact that there is good on both sides makes it all the more crucial to find the most accurate metaphor as the basis for the decision.

New metaphors are constantly arising — as they must, if metaphor is "one of the principal mechanisms of imaginative cognition"[53] and central to moral thinking. Johnson nevertheless doubts the possibility of deliberately changing a root cultural metaphor. With the recognition of the metaphoric structure of moral understanding,

> we have the means to determine at what level a change of metaphor (and thus a different moral understanding) might be possible. This will be a matter of how cognitively well entrenched a certain metaphor system is. The more basic a conceptual metaphor is, the more it will be systematically connected to other metaphors, and the more implications it will have for our moral reasoning. It is highly unlikely that our deepest metaphors can be changed, since the resultant cognitive disruption would be extreme. This is not to deny that occasionally individuals and even cultures undergo such radical transformations, but only to note the emotional, social, and cultural costs of such large-scale change. Perhaps the imposition of Western modes of experience on non-Western peoples is the most obvious example of such catastrophic change.[54]

By this analogy, the cost of uprooting the old God-language and imposing by fiat a new one, however superficially preferable it may be for valid political reasons, may be high. So far as Otto's model of the mutual attraction of ideas is accurate, not all ideas attract all ideas; to cut the existing lines of connection, or to forbid certain connections to be made, is to fragment the cultural consciousness, and not only traditionalists are right in seeing it as an act of war. Revisions that uproot the old God-language detach the language of liturgy even from the cultural sense of humor, where the male God with the beard will certainly continue to thrive; this is surely a mistake and will further limit the relevance of religion, not increase it. Those who impose new language naturally believe that the benefit far outweighs the cost, but if the new language repels connection with other ideas it will reduce the coherence of the culture it claims to serve.

Scheffler takes a more optimistic view of the ability of connections to survive, because they are reinforced at so many points; no conscious strategy of severance can find all the unconscious links.

> The strength of ritual may lie just in its being anchored by multiple referential bonds to objects. When one or more are cut, the others meanwhile hold fast. When one requires relocation under a new interpretive idea, the untying and retying process does not destroy the whole linkage. Thus it is that rituals change more slowly than creeds, often surviving even drastic alterations of doctrine and entering into new interpretive contexts without loss of vigor.[55]

This analysis might be encouraging — as might Staal's observation of the similarities between ritual and syntax — except that something depends on the worth of the "new interpretive idea": an idea with neither a filial nor an aesthetic attachment to the past makes for a less intelligible pattern. It can genuinely destroy associative connections, which may take decades or centuries to reestablish themselves in another place, or may never reestablish themselves. At every point where connections are lost, there is the possibility of ignorance, and perhaps of consequent bloodshed. Moral cognition and moral emotion have more to work with when religious language permits attraction between ideas; they have a far weaker hold among people with fewer and more atomized ideas (even when those are very strong ideas of what is "moral," on the left or the right). An idea that preserves the past intact, even while refusing its authority, is preferable to an idea that erases the past in order to break its power.

Ratey makes it clear[56] that the making of connections is neurological work; the brain, faced with a challenge either physical or mental, establishes firing patterns among neurons that allow thought, learning, kinetic memory and social connection to take place. Those who are compelled to think harder develop their intelligence farther; the simplification of liturgy or any other form of learning does its constituency no favor. Analogy is not always easy work; it may be ambiguous, it may be morally troubling. But it is the mind's method of exercise.

Verfremdung

Associative activity — which is simultaneously intellectual play and the most serious kind of emotional work — accomplishes something else whose importance to liturgy should not be underestimated. It is startling: it casts a new light on the habitual and taken-for-granted. The overlaying of one cognitive map on another is a re-cognition, in both the opposing senses of unexpected familiarity and sheer unexpectedness. Scheffler's "feeling of surprise" — which may, of course, be either pleasant or unpleasant surprise — is an essential cognitive emotion in liturgical life. Language designed for repetition must build in a certain intractable strangeness; it must not simply startle the first time (as, for example, "God the Mother" in place of "God the Father") but must continue to startle for centuries and millennia (like the male God's "I will howl like a woman in labor"[57]). Just as the hostile metaphor has a place, though not a comfortable place, in human discourse, strangeness and even estrangement have a place in our relationship with the numinous.

Bertolt Brecht's word *Verfremdung* — "strangeifying," alienation — is worth introducing here. Brecht's objection to naturalistic theater was that it hung everything on empathy: on the collapsing of distinctions between actor and character, between character and audience, between the stage set and an ordinary room. He insisted that theater was an art of otherness and ought to emphasize these distinctions. Distancing effects — whether stage conventions like the Greek chorus or deliberate assaults on the theatrical illusion like the exposure of lighting and sound-effect sources — take the audience out of daily life and transform experience; Brecht's productions leaned heavily on these effects. The *Verfremdungseffekt*, as he saw it,

> consists in turning the object of which one is to be made aware, to which one's attention is to be drawn, from something ordinary, familiar, immediately accessible, into something peculiar, striking and unexpected. What is obvious is in a certain sense made incomprehensible, but this is only in order that it may then be made all the easier to comprehend. Before familiarity can turn into awareness the familiar must be stripped of its inconspicuousness; we must give up assuming that the object in question needs no explanation.[58]

Brecht's source for the concept of *Verfremdung* was the Russian critic Victor Shklovsky's term *pryem ostranneniya* ("device for making strange").[59] In his 1917 essay "Art as Technique" Shklovsky argued against Symbolist criticism, whose ruling assumption was that "Art is thinking in images" which "clarify the unknown by means of the known,"[60] asserting instead that the purpose of art is to defamiliarize or "deautomatize" our surroundings. Shklovsky considered the Symbolist view facile; the sense of art as primarily symbolic could handle easily digestible imagery, but was unable to account for the more striking peculiarities of poetic language. Strangeness, he believed, could combat habitual perception, whose "algebraic" abbreviation of words and thoughts into a schematic form inevitably becomes a trained inattention in which we go about our daily business only half-aware. Art must rough up the perceptions in order to restore the capacity for sustained attention:

> Habitualization devours works, clothes, furniture, one's wife, and the fear of war....And art exists that one may recover the sensation of life; it exists to make one feel things, to make the stone *stony*. The purpose of art is to impart the sensation of things as they are perceived and not as they are known. The technique of art is to make objects "unfamiliar," to make forms difficult, to increase the difficulty and length of perception *because the process of perception is an aesthetic end in itself and must be prolonged.*[61]

For liturgical as well as artistic purposes it is important to note that defamiliarization is not simply a sudden shock that leaves the participant stranded in strange territory without help. It is a *slowed*, *sustained* shock, drawn out by the techniques of artistic difficulty to keep the perception both naked and focused for an increasing length of time. Shklovsky notes a number of poetic techniques to prolong the attention, including the use of arresting diction (usually either the archaic or the demotic), the roughening of the poetic line through variations in rhythm, and the enjambment of consonants to slow the pronunciation. He distinguishes between the effects of prose rhythm and poetic rhythm: prose rhythm (which imposes a pattern on a free form) is automatizing, and poetic rhythm (whose regularity would become tedious without "roughening" variations) is deautomatizing:

> The rhythm of prose, or of a work song...permits the members to do their necessary "groaning together" and also eases

the work by making it automatic. And, in fact, it is easier to march with music than without it, and to march during an animated conversation is even easier, for the walking is done unconsciously. Thus the rhythm of prose is an important automatizing element; the rhythm of poetry is not.... Should the disordering of [poetic] rhythm become a convention, it would be ineffective as a device for the roughening of language.[62]

Applied to liturgy, this points to the double need for stability and instability: the need for groaning *together*, in a predictable ritual form that we know well, with the sense of being upheld by compassionate others — but *groaning* together, without comforting euphemisms and with no refuge from the truth. The rhythms lull while the meanings unsettle.

There is, of course, a spontaneous *Verfremdung* as well as an induced one; it can be brought on by culture clash, abrupt movement between levels of daily living, or simply a sense of inner estrangement. Tolstoy's peculiar and comic description of an opera in *War and Peace*, which Shklovsky quotes at length in his essay, shows such an estrangement through a character's eyes (Natasha, newly arrived in Moscow and preoccupied by the uncertainty of her relations with her fiancé's family, and about to be drawn into a disastrous flirtation):

Maidens in red bodices and white skirts sat on the middle of the stage. One, very fat, in a white silk dress, sat apart on a narrow bench to which a green pasteboard box was glued from behind. They were all singing something. When they had finished, the maiden in white approached the prompter's box. A man in silk with tight-fitting pants on his fat legs approached her with a plume and began to sing and spread his arms in dismay. The man in the tight pants finished his song alone; then the girl sang. After that both remained

silent as the music resounded; and the man, obviously waiting to begin singing his part with her again, began to run
his fingers over the hand of the girl in the white dress. They
finished their song together, and everyone in the theater began to clap and shout.[63]

Shklovsky quotes the passage to show Tolstoy's use of defamiliarization as a narrative method — and might as easily have quoted
the second epilogue to *War and Peace*, where the technique appears
equally strikingly as political analysis: "At the end of the eighteenth
century there were some two dozen men in Paris who were beginning to talk about all men being free and equal. Because of this all
through France men fell to slashing and slaughtering one another."
But authorial method is generally a conscious application of the personality the author is stuck with, and Tolstoy was no stranger to
the experience of alienation. In middle age he endured a bleak and
suicidal period in which his desire to live was withdrawn, in which
he found himself "hiding the rope in order not to hang myself to the
rafters of the room where every night I went to sleep alone"[64] because
his life seemed incurably vacant of purpose or vibrancy. William
James cites him among other sufferers from depression as having had
an experience of transformation as intense as a religious conversion,
but in the negative: not the infusion but the draining out of meaning from the world. The desperate descriptions of mental patients
supplement James's account: "I see everything through a cloud,"
"a thick veil alters the hue and look of everything," "as if people
were actors, and everything were scenery," "I weep false tears, I have
unreal hands."[65] "Deautomatization" can be either better or worse
than habitual perception; at its worst, it shows people and things as
automata, animated perhaps by an intricate functioning structure
of bones and veins and nerves but pointless in their animation, un-
connected to the observer who must nonetheless go on observing
them. Isak Dinesen's character who defines man as "a minutely set,

ingenious machine for turning, with infinite artfulness, the red wine of Shiraz into urine"[66] must have known this state of mind.

At the opposite pole to this intense unrealness is the intense realness of the mystic's illumination. Arthur J. Deikman, in an article on "Deautomatization and the Mystic Experience," speculates that the ineffability of the mystical state is based on one of two factors: the mystic's proscription of analytic thought, which places the experience outside ordinary description; or else the sheer cognitive complexity of the revelation, which presents an associative network perceived all at once, beyond the resources of consecutive language. In liturgy both factors may operate: analytic thought flatly stated is certainly fatal to emotional connection, but also liturgy may layer and link its associative echoes until their resonances build and overwhelm. Deikman is interested mainly in traditional techniques of contemplation and renunciation; he recognizes that spontaneous mystical states do occur in the "untrained-sensate" (like James's informants) and in users of LSD, but he makes the conventional assumption that the traditional "way of negation" is the only fully developed path to mystical experience. But poetry, music, visual arts and theater are essentially techniques of contemplation and forms of training for the "untrained-sensate"; anyone who has felt the field of vision narrow and the air become charged with energy at an intense moment in a play or a concert, anyone who has walked around a sculpture to know it from every angle, has experienced what Deikman calls perceptual concentration.[67] Shklovsky's technique of "increas[ing] the difficulty and length of perception because the process of perception is an aesthetic end in itself and must be prolonged" is the artistic equivalent of chanting a mantra or staring at an icon or a candleflame, except that it starts with the aim of filling rather than emptying the mind. Art arrives at associative overload by a direct route, negative contemplation by an indirect.

Not incidentally, poetry, music and theater are the elements of liturgy; they increase the difficulty and length of perception because the process of perception is a *religious* end (which is never entirely an end in itself) and must be prolonged. If the child's cognition is concerned with assembling language and intellect to solve problems, and eventually brings language and intellect to bear on each other as thought, adult cognition is concerned with bringing thought and feeling to bear on each other in order to assist moral coherence. Defamiliarization, the deliberate destruction of habitual patterns of thought, is essential in this process. Private speech, as it survives into adult life in the liturgical monotone, remains a means of self-guidance or problem-solving, but the problem is not clearly soluble, or is soluble in more than one way. In a sense the slowing of perception serves to return us to a pre-habituated, childhood cognition; the New Testament saying that you must become as a little child to enter the kingdom of heaven[68] is not a nostalgia for innocence but a call for sharper perception. The child's task, which is complex and not wholly conscious, is to learn thought and language in preparation for adult life. At the adult level the task has become conscious, and has increased in complexity so far as to constitute one's whole errand on earth.

Chapter 3

"A Good Mouth-Filling Oath":
Early Modern Style

HOTSPUR. Heart, you swear like a comfit-maker's wife. "Not you, in good sooth!" and "as true as I live!" and "as God shall mend me!" and "as sure as day!"...

> Sweare me Kate, like a lady as thou art,
> A good mouth-filling oath.
> —Shakespeare, *Henry IV, Part One,* 3.i.

Those who object to the 'artificiality' of Milton or Dryden sometimes tell us to 'look into our hearts and write.' But that is not looking deep enough; Racine or Donne look into a good deal more than the heart. One must look into the cerebral cortex, the nervous system, and the digestive tracts.

> —T. S. Eliot, "The Metaphysical Poets"

Cognition is not only an associative process in which resemblances are perceived across apparent barriers of dissimilarity. It is also a process of judgment. As we might expect from an analogical system, not all the brain's judgments are based on pure reason; the amygdala, a structure in the limbic system, has been identified as the source of a kind of emotional assessment so fundamental that we generally take it for granted, which Ratey calls "the cognitive process of assigning emotional weight to perceptions."[1] The amygdala "provides a pre-conscious bias of intensity to every stimulus"[2] before that stimulus ever reaches the frontal lobes for reasoned analysis. It tells us whether an event is worth taking notice of, interrupting ourselves for, getting out of the way of. In a crisis, the amygdala governs the fight-or-flight response, and its judgments are instantaneous; it affects the quality of our attention before we begin to attend.

How verbal the amygdala is — whether it can distinguish the emotional weight of "cry unto her that her warfare is accomplished, that her iniquity is pardoned, that she hath received of the Lord's hand double for all her sins"[3] from that of "I rejoiced whenever people said to me, let's journey to the house of THE UNSEEN!" — is a question that seems not to have attracted researchers thus far. The amygdala is thought to provide "meaning," in the form of mood, for the random events of life that the frontal cortex then gathers into narrative coherence.[4] If it can do that, it may be able to recognize the urgency or placidity of a statement, its directness or circumlocution, its genuine emotion or its bland simulation of sincerity. Every student, and every congregant, knows there are words that compel attention and words that make you sink deeper into your chair, and nobody has any trouble telling which is which; the neural mechanism remains to be studied, but the experience is well enough known. The frontal cortex may certainly decode and find great significance in a rational statement that the amygdala has found merely tedious; we are versatile enough to do several kinds of work for our knowledge, and emotional work is only one of them. But in speech meant for frequent repetition it is as well to have the brain's arbiter of emotional weight on your side.

"O, but they say the tongues of dying men / Enforce attention like deep harmony."[5] Early modern English — the English of the sixteenth and early seventeenth centuries — produced a liturgical language that still carries enormous emotional weight. Even in a time that has largely discarded the old Book of Common Prayer and the King James Bible from liturgical practice, phrases from both sources, as from Shakespeare, persist in our common speech. Many of them date back to pre-King Jamesian biblical translations, and a few to liturgies first written in Middle English. The sense of a time long past and a language underlying one's own is part of the appeal of an old liturgy — for those to whom it appeals; the direst defamiliarization, the defamiliarization from life, adds a poignant strangeness to old words and expressions. But early modern religious language bears the marks of an additional stress. The threat of martyrdom hangs over all the early Protestant writings, and concentrates them; writers who could die for their theology, or even for translating the Bible, "meant what they said" in a sense that present-day liturgists do not dream of.

William Tyndale, first translator of the Bible into English from the original Hebrew and Greek rather than Latin, worked in exile and was executed in 1536, having evolved a style that would have enormous influence (though he left the Hebrew Bible half finished, having begun with the New Testament). Thomas Cranmer, Henry VIII's Archbishop of Canterbury and editor of the first Book of Common Prayer, was burned for heresy in 1556, having established a style noted ever since for its sobriety and resonance. Miles Coverdale, who finished Tyndale's work (less expertly, working at first from German and Latin models and later learning some Hebrew), and whose psalm translations were retained by the Book of Common Prayer until the 1970s, endured repeated periods of exile and poverty until his death from old age in 1569.[6] Hebrew has endured for three millennia the recurrent shocks of persecution and loss; early modern English — influenced by Hebrew both imaginatively and syntactically — survived the Reformation in the Bible and Protestant liturgy with a strength which for four hundred years seemed unshakable. In fact in secular usage it has not been shaken; even now that its fragility has been conclusively demonstrated in the religious realm by recent translations and liturgies, "God's lively word" is still lively in every realm but religion. As a theological idiom its range has narrowed considerably — a circumstance not everyone would lament; as a linguistic force it is virtually undiminished.

The sixteenth century was the linguistic flashpoint of English culture; largely because of political developments begun at that point, English is (for better or for worse) the global language of our time. Whatever we think of the British Empire, our own vernacular got its start along with it: our languages of literature and science, diplomacy and scholarship, advertising and popular music, trace back to the time of Henry VIII and Elizabeth I. The sixteenth century was also a liturgical flashpoint in Western Christianity; the theological ferment that had been working since the heretical movements of the thirteenth century, and which bubbled up uncontainably with the introduction of the printing press, was among other things a demand for religion in the language of the people. Every major European vernacular had a Bible before English (England having outlawed biblical translation after the Wyclif Bible of the early 1380s, with its connection to the Peasants' Revolt); perhaps that circumstance particularly intensified the English translations. Vernacular liturgy was a more complex matter than vernacular Bibles, since it involved the establishment of a new public practice; Cranmer's liturgy was not simply a translation of the Latin but a substantial revision of Roman rites both theologically and practically, designed to reduce pageantry, eliminate intercessory prayer, and present a radically different definition of the communion. Those who resented his innovations may have done so for a mixture of theological and aesthetic reasons, but it seems unlikely that anyone of Cranmer's own party would have thought his approach lightweight.

The vernacular is a perennial crisis point in religious language. The authority of scripture in a foreign, authoritative language puts heavy pressure on a provincial language that may have no terminology for the central concepts of the religion. The translator is charged, essentially, with creating a new vocabulary of salvation. In translating from a developed language into an undeveloped one, the writer creates a hybrid speech from any available materials — *growing* the language by an infusion from another source, while recombining its existing elements. Thus translation is naturally a site of linguistic change, especially translation into a language in which there is virtually no scholarship and no substantial body of literature. Martin Luther's Bible influenced German vocabulary and syntax decisively; Tyndale's, especially as it was absorbed into the King James Bible, did the same in English. (The Jewish Enlightenment, particularly in the late nineteenth and early twentieth centuries, provides an interesting parallel in its counter-movement toward secularity. The Yiddish literary scene of the early twentieth century used translation as a testing ground for aesthetic and psychological innovations unthinkable to the religious and socialist pieties of earlier generations; the first modern Hebrew writers lamented the artificiality of using the biblical vocabulary for secular narrative. To create, as it were, a vernacular out of the holy tongue is as arduous as rendering the holy tongue into a new vernacular.) The effort to stretch a language to accommodate the Bible alters it permanently; the vernacular gives birth to a book begotten upon it by another language and culture, and its shape is visibly changed.

Translation may also introduce ideas that enter the new language without securely settling there. "Lovingkindness," Coverdale's effort to translate the Hebrew *ḥesed*, was absorbed into liturgy but attained no wider currency (possibly because the means of cultivating the behavior were so different between Jewish culture and Anglo-American culture, or possibly because four syllables are more unwieldy than two). "Carnal knowledge," derived from the Hebrew *daat*, became standard legal language, and students still approach the loss of their virginity with arch references to "knowledge in the biblical sense," but has English ever really absorbed the idea of sexual intercourse as a mode of *cognition*? Yet the haunting of the vernacular by such half-realized terms provides a sense of *Verfremdung* important to the moral imagination. Luther, always alert to a striking phrase in the Hebrew, noted in the preface to his translation of the Psalms that at certain points the available idiom of the host language cannot convey the novelty and force of the original, so that the peculiarity of the literal sense will serve better:

> But we have also sometimes translated word for word, though we could have done it otherwise and more clearly, and for this reason: the words have something important in them. Psalm 68:18, for example: "Thou art gone up on high, and hast led captivity captive." An idiomatic translation would be, "hast freed the prisoners." But that is too weak and does not yield the rich, subtle sense of the Hebrew. "Thou hast led captivity captive" — that is, not only has Christ released the prisoners, but he has in the process taken away the prison, taken it captive, so that it can never again take us prisoner, and our redemption is eternal....To honor such teaching, and for the comfort of our souls, we must retain such words, must put up with them, and so give the Hebrew some room where it does better than German can.[7]

Franz Rosenzweig, collaborating with Martin Buber on another German translation five hundred years later, was much struck by this comment; the Buber-Rosenzweig translation was radically unlike Luther's in its insistence on "giving the Hebrew some room" at every possible opportunity. (Everett Fox's contemporary translation *The Five Books of Moses* was made according to the Buber-Rosenzweig method; a comparison of Fox's text with the King James will give a sense of how strange Buber and Rosenzweig's translation was next to Luther's.) For Rosenzweig it was imperative to let "the genius of the alien language" be heard through the host language, as a kind of induction to the overwhelming and permanent strangeness of revelation. Most modern translators' preference for the idiomatic and immediately intelligible has heavily reduced the quotient of strangeness in their Bibles, making for a more superficially "accessible" text but putting the *Verfremdung* both of art and of revelation farther out of the reader's reach. The only exceptions are Harold Fisch's "Jerusalem Bible," published by the Israeli publisher Koren (not to be confused with the Catholic translation of the same name), which is essentially the King James Old Testament with the names in their Hebrew forms and the inaccuracies corrected; and various recent partial translations by literary writers: Robert Alter's *Five Books of Moses*, Mary Phil Korsak's *At the Start...Genesis Made New*, Stephen Mitchell's *Book of Job*, Reynolds Price's *A Palpable God* and *Three Gospels*, and Willis Barnstone's *New Covenant*, all of which work incisively toward defamiliarizing the text and none of which will ever appear in the pews for general use.

Tyndale's translations of the 1520s and '30s are noted, like Luther's, for their clarity and memorable phrasing. They were meant for a plain-speaking peasant readership — Tyndale famously said in an argument at the outset of his career, "If God spare my life, ere many years I will cause a boy that driveth the plough shall know more of the scripture than thou dost"[8] — but were widely read by all classes; Anne Boleyn's copy of Tyndale's New Testament still survives, with her name written on the edge. The Tyndale signatures are memorable phrases (let there be light, the powers that be, fight the good fight, a stranger in a strange land, a man after his own heart, the apple of his eye), plangent coinages for which there was no English equivalent (longsuffering, mercy seat, Passover, scapegoat, foreskin), and a speed so relentless as to make a translation almost a hundred years older than the King James seem far more modern. Hebrew syntax affected English syntax permanently through Tyndale's work: his rendering of the construct form — *ḥayat ha-aretz, dagat ha-yam, of ha-shamayim, malakh adonai, elohei avotenu* (the beasts of the earth, the fish of the sea, the fowl of the air, the angel of the Lord, God of our fathers) — gave the possessive form "of the" for the first time an equal billing with the inflected genitive (the earth's beasts, the sea's fish, the Lord's angel), and actually made it preferable for elevated language.[9] Tyndale's phrasing, freely taken into the King James translation, accounts for roughly 80 percent of the books of the Bible that he translated, according to a recent computer analysis.[10] His all-but-anonymous influence on what subsequent readers and hearers thought of as biblical language is ubiquitous.

What a cognitive scientist calls "emotional weight" a translator calls "register": the position of a word or phrase on the continuum of formal and colloquial, standard and nonstandard, serious and funny, erudite and vulgar, current and archaic, polite and obscene. David Daniell, editor of Tyndale's translations and polemical writings and author of a critical biography, has closely analyzed the register of Tyndale's prose and concluded that "part of his genius as a translator was his gift for knowing how ordinary people used language at slightly heightened moments, and translating at that level."[11] The slight heightening is what we no longer believe in; Daniell remarks that in replacing Tyndale's "Let not your hearts be troubled" with "Do not be worried or upset"[12] the *Good News Bible* translates "as if the disciples were being told by Jesus to cheer up after having missed a bus."[13] (They are dismayed at his announcement of his impending death.) One almost has the sense that such translations replace "slight heightening" with flat colloquialism because the translators are unmoved, or want the reader to be unmoved; heightening cannot quite be achieved in cold blood. ("Do not" scarcely counts as heightening, though no one says it in speaking; in the context it merely seems faintly sanctimonious. One of the more startling instances of this mix of the stilted and the colloquial is the Annotated Scholars Bible's rendering of Luke 1:34, Mary's "I know not a man," as "I've not had sex with any man."[14]) The range of the translator's emotions is really all that determines the subtle and successful negotiation of register. Writing is character: there are no shortcuts.

Where the King James departs from Tyndale's text, it is sometimes to become *unnecessarily* heightened; the translation was "appointed to be read in churches" rather than smuggled into England in bales of wool and concealed under cottage floorboards. Tyndale's speed is so direct and urgent as to become unseemly in an ecclesiastical hierarchy. But the King James is more radical than Tyndale in reproducing the paratactic, the use of *and* at the beginnings of sentences, a usage that became indelibly "biblical" in the common memory. The *and* has paradoxical effects: even as it serves as a clear marker of elevated style, it reaches back into an oral narrative past in which most sentences hook themselves to the previous sentences, a habit which the most casual teenage speech preserves to this day. ("And she goes, 'Do you think she had sex with him?' And I go, 'I dunno, she's been looking kind of green for about a month.' And she was like, 'No!'"). Students are still told by their high school teachers never to begin a sentence with *and*, so a certain heady mixture of religiously mandated high formality and academically proscribed natural speech is implicit in the syntax itself. Though the conjunction *ve-* in Hebrew certainly serves a range of purposes, its retention as *and* in English underlines certain attractive aspects of biblical prose: its mix of elevation and intimacy, bedrock stability and radical surprise, authority and transgression.

And when intensified experience lays hold on us, the language comes back. One can observe the sudden tightening of the prose in students' first-semester compositions when they speak of death or moral resolution or some experience of the numinous; most students will rise to dignity fairly readily when excused from the duty of glibness, and some of the least expertly literate have the most striking command. One community college student whose writing was generally awkward and undistinguished responded to Elias Canetti's cryptic aphorism "Men's voices are God's bread"[15] by saying that when we speak to God "we plenish him"; it may have come from clandestine reading of Shakespeare or the dictionary, it may have been the intuitive reinvention of an obsolete word, but he knew how to do it. A newspaper columnist noted with astonishment that New York adolescents after the destruction of the World Trade Center spoke without the perpetual interpolation "like", as if "like" were an uncontrollable tic and not a deliberate marker of casualness in conversation.[16] "A formal feeling comes": people do know the relative gravity of their circumstances, and if they speak casually while shopping or working or talking idly on the phone, they have simply gauged accurately that they are in a situation that makes no demands. Generally they still imagine situations that do make demands, and practice in secret the language of those situations — not simply a private but even a furtive speech.

Walter Mitty and Miniver Cheevy notwithstanding, there is no reason to mock or discourage the tendency; it can be approached with linguistic expertise and critical discipline. A culture in which *The Lord of the Rings* has become staple reading for older children has no problem with heightened language, some of it considerably predating the sixteenth century; the next generation of liturgists may well take for granted the general currency of Tolkien's style. The survival of King Jamesian language in gospel music also makes clear that the active vocabulary of religion transcends the supposed verbal limitations of the popular audience. What makes the words irreplaceable is not so much their age as their emotional topography: *mercy, burden, glory*. There is no reason to put old language off limits to new writers; all language, in the end, is judged not by its archaism or currency but by its integrity.

A slight heightening does not mean a sanctimonious reverence — often the last habit to hang on in a liturgist's style when the last ounce of emotional weight has been cast away; it means having a feel for the topography. Current readers, understandably enough, cannot always distinguish between the sixteenth century's use of an expression and the nineteenth's; what was a slight heightening to Tyndale in 1530 became an awful loftiness among the Anglican clergy of Tennyson's time. Solemnity naturally tends to increase exponentially as conviction gives way to overcompensation. Conviction results in a certain matter-of-factness; an age of conviction, even when it is at home with heightened language, is as likely to be barbed and satirical as to be reverent. Sixteenth-century Protestantism supplemented genuine awe for God with earthy humor and a calculated irreverence toward God's ecclesiastical chain of command, and metaphor surfaces in the theological writing of the time in wildly unedifying ways. The Reformation polemicists — starting with Luther, whose scatological invention is the stuff of legend — had no sense of propriety in our terms; where a present-day academic theologian would face her intellectual foes armed with sober reasoning and the names and terminology of eminent theorists, the Reformers hit out in all directions like intellectual berserkers. The nature of the Eucharist, one of the acute crisis points of the theology of the time, was a favorite topic of homely simile:

> Alas! that men consider nothing at all, how that the coupling of Christ's body and blood to the sacrament is a spiritual thing; and therefore there needs be no such carnal presence as the papists imagine. Who will deny a man's wife to be with her husband one body and flesh, although he be at London and she at York?[17]

> If when thou seest the sacrament or eateth [*sic*] his body or drinkest his blood, thou have this promise fast in thine heart (that his body was slain and his blood shed for thy sins) and believest it, so thou art saved and justified thereby. If not, so it helpeth thee not, though thou hearest a thousand masses in a day or though thou doest nothing else all thy life long, than eat his body or drink his blood: no more than it should help thee in a dead thirst, to behold a bush at a tavern door, if thou knewest not thereby that there were wine within to be sold.[18]

At full deployment, the metaphors could hit below the belt: here is Tyndale defending the literal reading of scripture as against the allegorical method long current in Catholicism, which the Protestant sensibility found fantastical:

> Likewise in the homely gest of Noah, when he was drunk, and lay in his tent with his privy members open, hast thou great edifying in the literal sense. Thou seest what became of the cursed children of wicked Ham which saw his father's privy members and jested thereof to his brethren. Thou seest also what blessing fell on Shem and Japhet which went backward and covered their father's members and saw them not. And thirdly thou seest what infirmity accompanies God's elect be they never so holy, which is yet not imputed unto them [i.e., is not counted against them in God's judgment]. For the faith and trust they have in God swalloweth up all their sins.
>
> Notwithstanding this text offereth us an apt and handsome allegory or similitude to describe our wicked Ham, Antichrist the Pope, which many hundred years hath done all the shame that heart can think of unto the privy member of God which is the word of promise or the word of faith as Paul calleth it and the gospel and testament of Christ wherewith we are begotten[.][19]

Tyndale's logic slips here — how does the Pope recapitulate Ham's sin by *concealing*, rather than exposing, scripture? — but the image of scripture as "the privy member of God...wherewith we are begotten" is worth the lapse. (It is also consonant with some kabbalistic metaphors for the Torah scroll, though there is no telling whether Tyndale could have known it.)

In this freewheeling invective there is something utterly out of keeping with what we now take to be the terms of theological debate. There is no subdued collegialism, no inhibition of impulse, no rationality except the rough-and-ready reasoning needed to prove a point. The emotional amplitude is more closely akin to Shakespearean abuse:

OSWALD. This ancient ruffian, sir, whose life I have spared at suit of his gray beard —
KENT. Thou whoreson zed, thou unnecessary letter! My lord, if you will give me leave, I will tread this unbolted villain into mortar and daub the walls of a jakes with him. Spare my gray beard! you wagtail.[20]

Of course verbal abuse at this level is not found in liturgy. The Book of Common Prayer pursues its theological agenda more subtly; Cranmer's capital theological offense was his description of the Eucharist as a "memorial," which for later generations sits with unremarkable sedateness in his communion service. ("And did institute, and in his holy Gospel command us to continue, a perpetual memory of that his precious death and sacrifice"; "the memorial thy Son hath commanded us to make.") But in an unpublished counter-polemic against the Catholic rebels in Devon and Cornwall Cranmer made "a scatological joke about St. Martin and the Devil which the Archbishop's Victorian editor found too appalling to print in full,"[21] and even while imprisoned for heresy said tartly in an appeal that "the bishop of Rome (whom they call Pope)...hath authority of God, yet by that power or authority he is not become unsinnable...if he shall command any thing that is not right to be done, he ought to take it patiently and in good part, in case he be not therein obeyed."[22] It is worth mulling over the relationship between invective and the language of ardor; it may be that the writer needs access to the full range. The mind that can write "I smell all horsepiss"[23] is the mind that can write "poor old heart, he holp the heavens to rain;"[24] the Tyndale of "God's privy member" is the Tyndale of "Let not your hearts be troubled." When liturgy becomes a civilized art, for which one can no longer die at the stake, perhaps it must still maintain its links to the scatological.

Orality and Literacy

Early modern English lived on the cusp between oral and written language. Wide literacy was a new phenomenon, directly tied to the Reformation — people learned to read in order to read the vernacular Bibles — and written prose was still meant for the ear more than the eye. Cranmer's prose in the Book of Common Prayer is slower and more erudite than Tyndale's deliberately direct syntax — the subordinate clauses presuppose a literate eye for the referent — but the listener has no trouble keeping track of the referent or sorting out the subordinate clauses. Eloquence was a spoken as well as a written art, meant for intelligent listening; the illiterate had trained ears, and used them.

Walter J. Ong, in *Orality and Literacy*, notes the prevalence of proverbs and clichés in oral language. The pithy saying is brief and memorable, not too strikingly original, and self-reinforcing by being satisfying to repeat: "A stitch in time saves nine," "Don't count your chickens before they're hatched," "Waste not want not," "Curiosity killed the cat." The strength of oral language is its architecture: its rhymes and near-rhymes, its repetition of forms or phonemes, its syntactical patterns (including subordinate clauses). Without these, memory would be lost in finding its way through experience. In a culture where all thought must be retained in memory in order to survive, Ong points out, you must "think memorable thoughts":

> In a primary oral culture, to solve effectively the problem of retaining and retrieving carefully articulated thought, you have to do your thinking in mnemonic patterns, shaped for ready oral recurrence. Your thought must come into being in heavily rhythmic, balanced patterns, in repetitions or antitheses, in alliterations and assonances, in epithetic and other formulary expressions...in proverbs which are constantly heard by everyone so that they come to mind readily and which themselves are patterned for retention and ready

recall, or in other mnemonic form. Serious thought is intertwined with memory systems. Mnemonic needs determine
even syntax.[25]

A thought without pattern would be unretainable; "[i]t would
not be abiding knowledge but simply a passing thought, however
complex."[26]

A contemporary parallel is in the catch-phrases that reach us
through television and our friends, so that suddenly everyone is saying "No way!" (closely followed by "Way!"), "Sounds like a plan,"
"That's why they pay me the big bucks," "Not the brightest bulb
on the Christmas tree," "One sick puppy." Alcoholics Anonymous
slogans — "Get off the pity pot," "I'd rather have a bottle in front
of me than a frontal lobotomy," "Let go and let God," "Denial isn't
just a river in Egypt" — have the full complement of oral-language
features. As a benign form of social cohesion this kind of talk is
pleasant and companionable, and sometimes happily ironic; as an
evasion of life below the emotional surface it can be exasperating.
Anyone whose mother or grandmother had a good stock of proverbs
knows what it is to be rebuffed with one. Ultimately the AA slogans
have the same quality of brisk dismissal in the guise of insight.

The limitation of oral language is its predictability. Even the
new catch-phrase ("A can of worms," "You don't want to go there")
introduces only a grain of newness, and the mood behind it repels
any deeper intimacy. Habituation does make for good pedagogy; it
certainly preserves (and even compels) privacy; in ballads and epic
poems it supplies a repetition that is deeply grounding. One does
not get bored with "the wine-dark sea" or "'twas in the merry month
of May," which are necessary inductions. But habit, however intertwined with serious thought, does not encourage the exploration of
previously unexplored mental territory.

What literacy introduces into a language is the permanent possibility of the unpredictable: new, formerly unimagined modes of

expression for what had been inarticulate nuances of experience. "Unaccommodated man," that "poor, bare, forked animal,"[27] is not the stuff of tried-and-true common sense; it is a sudden view, as if by lightning, of the nature of destitution, so painful that it cannot become a proverb. When such a phrase enters the oral stock, it does so as literary allusion — an element in a new cultural store of potent understanding, all of it retrievable from written texts and attributable to particular authors. "A rose by any other name would smell as sweet"[28] *has* become a proverb, but it says less; it fits comfortably into the complacencies of casual conversation (and maternal rebuff) and does not quite need attribution. The more unusual phrase — with the higher quotient of *Verfremdung* — is striking enough that it will always seem the product of a particular mind, to which the culture owes a particular debt.

A literate person speaks differently, even when speaking extemporaneously, than an unlettered one. At the same time, in a primarily literate culture the illiterate or uncertainly literate will absorb some of the habits of literacy by hearing them used aloud. (This happens, for instance, in a marriage between a reader and a non-reader over the course of decades.) Where Vygotsky asserts that writing entails "deliberate structuring of the web of meaning," Ong says that writing "restructures thought,"[29] even "restructures consciousness"[30] — and not only the consciousness of the writer, but of the reader and the reader's eventual hearers, in widening circles. The isolation of writing, its withdrawal from social bonds and habits, ripples outward into a new social coherence:

> The highly interiorized stages of consciousness in which the individual is not so immersed unconsciously in communal structures are stages which, it appears, consciousness would never reach without writing. The interaction between the orality that all human beings are born into and the technology of writing, which no one is born into, touches the

depths of the psyche. Ontogenetically and phylogenetically, it is the oral word that first illuminates consciousness with articulate language...and that ties human beings to one another in society. Writing introduces division and alienation, but a higher unity as well. It intensifies the sense of self and fosters more conscious interaction between persons. Writing is consciousness-raising.[31]

In liturgy, which is simultaneously a written and an oral form, "serious thought is intertwined with memory systems" in a qualitatively different sense than in an oral culture. It is literate in the sense that it can support original language and complex trains of syntax and thought; it is oral in the sense that this more complex language lends itself to absorption into the memory. The synthesis is peculiarly powerful: it allows the stability of oral language with the addition of a disquieting consciousness just outside the group's. It is gradually accessible to young listeners as they advance in cognitive capacity, and available to adults at full strength as the need arises. It is always one step ahead of the congregation by using language slightly above the casual register. It makes possible both an introspection and a kind of mutual presence that could not otherwise evolve; it restructures the consciousness of the whole community.

Speech, obviously, can exist without writing — though writing adds a dimension that oral cultures generally find desirable, even as it brings with it a poignant sense of lost mental and social patterns. But writing "can never dispense with orality."[32] Language itself is fundamentally speech. Orality is persistent, incurable; it is bodily, and if liturgy is to stand up to repetition it must work with the body. When it tries to impose a raised consciousness by physically unwelcome means it will be resisted, and its carefully rationalized lessons will not even be remembered unless to be mocked. "Rhythm aids recall, even physiologically"[33]; it is the language written for the needs of the ear, not the language that makes the correct point in words indifferent to the ear, that will surface at moments of crisis to steady the mind and inform the judgment. It don't mean a thing if it ain't got that swing: if you cannot establish your principles in language worth remembering, you cannot firmly establish them.

The education of sixteenth-century writers aimed to elevate the skills of the average writer and speaker to a high level of competence, and to bring the writer of genius to the particular form of perfection that only he (it was, of course, generally *he*) could achieve. Erasmus, in his 1512 textbook *De utraque verborem ac rerum copia — De copia* for short — exercised his students' wits by demonstrating a hundred and fifty ways of saying "Your letter pleased me very much,"[34] and requiring similar verbal feats of them. One cannot attempt varied eloquence on such a scale without discovering something about register. In the hands of an unimaginative sycophant, such an exercise can produce an infinite series of florid, empty compliments; in the hands of a skilled and feeling writer it could produce — Shakespeare. Ong remarks that *copia* "could be exploited at all cognitive levels, sensory and intellectual simultaneously"[35]; in a culture where orality and literacy were still closely linked, it was a useful means of learning one's way around language. It was "elite" education, but only because the elite were in a position to buy it; one need not experience the rigor of Erasmus's drill at first hand to grasp the possibilities of prodigious inventiveness. Anyone who is interested can replicate the drill at home or in slow times at work; the learning is in the doing.

Elite young men of the sixteenth century were encouraged to leave some work for their readers to do; the mutual exercise of intelligence was a facet of courtesy. Erasmus said in *De Copia* that "things should not be written in such a way that everyone understands everything, but so that they are forced to investigate certain things, and learn."[36] This open-endedness was bound up with the emphasis on rhetoric in medieval and Renaissance universities[37]: the agonistic oral debate, conducted as a battle of ideas whose outcome was always in doubt. "Orality situates knowledge in a context of struggle"[38]; spoken thought is not abstract but emotionally charged. No doubt this accounts for the high pitch of Reformation polemic, but a thought with an emotional charge is more likely in any age to have an immediate cognitive appeal. Recalling Mark Johnson's definition of moral decision-making as the construction of a narrative with an *agon* that must be resolved, a thought that arises as if by necessity creates a sense of coherence; it employs the whole mind, so that we go on thinking compulsively. Uncertainty adds immeasurably to the thought's power; we are not passive recipients of a settled interpretation, but agents whose thoughts and acts have consequences. Repetition does not make the thought tedious, but conveys a deepening sense of the *agon's* continued distance from resolution.

For all the power of the printing press in spreading Reformation literacy, the primary text of Reformation literacy — the New Testament — was the record of a man who taught in parables; its orality was assured in its very structure. But it was also a document of the "people of the book," for whom written language was as fundamental as speech. The struggle with and for the text is one of its central preoccupations. "You have heard it said, An eye for an eye and a tooth for a tooth; but I say unto you, Resist not evil."[39] "And he closed the book...and he began to say unto them, This day is this scripture fulfilled in your ears."[40] The *agon* between Christianity and Judaism remains unresolved; despite the best efforts of both religions to keep it under control, it is written into the New Testament. But both religions share powerful assumptions about language, expressed through metaphors that converge and diverge: that the world was made through words; that God is known essentially by his words (whether the touchstone of that knowledge is *Hear O Israel* or *The Word was made flesh and dwelt among us*); that our own worthiness is judged by our words as well as our acts. *May the words of my mouth and the meditation of my heart be acceptable in thy sight*: it is not a sure thing that they will be. This uncertainty is the motive force of early modern English, for both religious and intellectual reasons.

Metamorphoses of the Sentence

Early modern syntax arose not only from the urgency of Reformers to get the Bible into the hands of the people, but from the anxiety of vernacular stylists about the adequacy of their native tongues. As the language of intellectual currency shifted from Latin to the vernaculars, the same problems had to be worked out in every European language: where to find a vocabulary for abstract thought, how to make fine conceptual and emotional distinctions that the oral languages had not previously needed, and how to construct a sentence in the language of daily living that would hold intellectual work. The etymological layering of English — the stark and often monosyllabic Anglo-Saxon, the softer French, the flood of Latinate neologisms in the sixteenth centuries — provides a particularly complex example,[41] but the difficulty was general. Certain literary stylists of the late sixteenth and early seventeenth centuries — sometimes still writing in Latin, sometimes in French or English — reacted against the elaborate, stately Ciceronian "period" that provided the model of oratorical eloquence, in favor of a shorter and more direct sentence. Their conscious influences were not biblical or liturgical — their acknowledged models were Seneca, Tacitus and Demosthenes — but in England the influence of the vernacular Bibles and the developing Anglican liturgy must have been so pervasive as to need no conscious acknowledgment. Morris Croll points out that the Ciceronian style was in any case only possible in a highly inflected language — any attempt to reproduce it in the minimally inflected vernaculars of Western Europe "must produce either fantastic distortion or insufferable bombast"[42]; the simpler and more consecutive grammatical structure of English or French required more immediacy. Tyndale had come to grips with this grammatical difference when he exclaimed that "the properties of the Hebrew tongue agreeth a thousand times more with the English than with the Latin. The manner of speaking is both one, so that in a thousand places thou needest not but to translate it into the English word for word."[43]

Croll's thinking about this stylistic development evolved over the course of a career, as did his names for it; from referring to it as the "anti-Ciceronian," "Attic," or "Senecan" style he eventually came to think of it as the "baroque" style, equivalent to concurrent developments in painting, sculpture and architecture. As Croll saw it, the thrust of humanist learning and Reformation piety toward introspection and independent judgment resulted in a drive to convey in its prose "the secret experiences of arduous and solitary minds, to express, even in the intricacies and subtleties of its form, the difficulties of a soul exploring unfamiliar truth by the unaided exercise of its own faculties."[44] The mind, made free of the realm of thought in the common tongue, was learning its way around doubt. Whatever one calls the new style — some critics have called it "libertine" — its writers aimed "to portray, not a thought, but a mind thinking":

> They knew that an idea separated from the act of experiencing it is not the idea that was experienced. The ardor of its conception in the mind is a necessary part of its truth; and unless it can be conveyed to another mind in something of the form of its occurrence, either it has changed into some other idea or it has ceased to be an idea, to have any existence whatever except a verbal one.…[They] deliberately chose as the moment of expression that in which the idea first clearly objectifies itself in the mind, in which, therefore, each of its parts still preserves its own peculiar emphasis and an independent vigor of its own — in brief, the moment in which truth is still *imagined*.[45]

The idea, thus caught at the point of emergence, remained attached to feeling and morally potent. The Reformation's acute sense of contingency — the contingency of spiritual authority, of institutional stability, of life itself in a theocratic state and in a time of plague — was stabilized and anchored by the conviction that spiritual authority could arise from within and that scientific method could inquire directly of nature. The new style employed a sort of across-the-board empiricism, at once religious and secular. Croll speaks of the "courageous skepticism and rhetorical audacity"[46] of the scientific and medical writers of the late sixteenth and early seventeenth centuries, who conducted as it were a kind of monotheistic search of the natural and moral orders for the one irreducible truth, the reproducible result.

> The ambition of [the leaders of seventeenth-century rationalism] — Lipsius, Montaigne, Bacon — was to conduct an experimental investigation of the moral realities of their time, and to achieve a style appropriate to the expression of their discoveries and of the mental effort by which they were conducted. The content of style became, as it were, suddenly greater and more difficult; and the stylistic formalities of the preceding age were unable to bear the burden.[47]

Written syntax began to break down; a sentence would wander off from one of its subordinate clauses into a new train of thought, or begin by taking one attitude toward a question and subtly undermine its own stance in the words that followed. It was an inductive and digressive style, each phrase giving rise to the next without ever knitting up the beginning of the sentence in the end. As one might expect of a mind thinking, it was associative and did not develop an argument efficiently. Nonetheless it never failed to keep emotional contact with the argument or leave work for the reader to do.

"As the [seventeenth] century advanced, however," Croll observes, "it became apparent that science was not to remain on the side of poetry and the imagination."[48] Contributing to this change was a radical shift in prose style, which would have repercussions everywhere: the ordering of grammar and syntax, and the beginning of systematic presentation as we still understand it. Even punctuation changed — for the better, from the point of view of clarity and visual organization, but often for the worse in terms of resonance and emotional subtlety. Punctuation had originally evolved for the reading voice, marking breath units and the duration of pauses; it was gradually standardized for print into a system of syntactic markers, which contributed to the speed of reading but undermined the ability to hear the words that one read.[49] The sense of prose still current among copy editors and writers of composition handbooks — the point-by-point outline, the paragraph mechanically organized around a topic sentence, the essay framed by an introduction and conclusion that repeat the main points of the body — originates in the attitudes of the late seventeenth and eighteenth centuries. The era introduced

> the study of the precise meaning of words; the reference to dictionaries as literary authorities; the study of the sentence as a logical unit alone; the careful circumscription of its limits and the gradual reduction of its length; the disappearance of semicolons and colons; the attempt to reduce grammar to an exact science; the idea that forms of speech are always either correct or incorrect; the complete subjection of the laws of motion and expression in style to the laws of logic and standardization — in short, the triumph, during two centuries, of grammatical over rhetorical ideas.[50]

It was a style and a register more suited to the didactic than the reflective; in certain ways it was inimical to the literary. It was firmly on the side of edification rather than discovery. It made an idea seem settled and teachable and routine, as if its conception in the mind had involved no ardor.

A major influence in this development came not from literary or scientific method but from pedagogy: a system, not altogether coherent but enormously popular, for organizing thought and writing. Peter Ramus (Pierre de la Ramée, 1515–1572) may be considered the progenitor of the textbook — if not quite the textbook as we now know it, leached of all possible controversial elements and too bland to hold anyone's interest, at least highly organized and without ambiguities. Ramus was not concerned with how to catch an idea at the point of emergence, but with how to impart ideas to a motley group of adolescents whose cognitive development and attention span were no doubt uneven and whose academic reading was chiefly the Greek and Latin philosophers and orators. Though he thought of his work as the development of a logical method, Ramus had, in Ong's judgment, "no real skill as a logician but only a blind drive toward a quantified approach to mental activity."[51] The Ramist method approached forms like oratory and poetry, with their essential oral qualities, as material to be "stripped down to its essentials" — that is, abstractions and syllogisms.[52] Style was opaque to Ramus; *copia* as a means of developing eloquence was simply irrelevant. His "plain style" "eliminat[ed] the vocal and personalist in favor of the diagrammatic."[53] The orderly presentation of argument was everything; the cast of the writer's mind was merely a sort of static or interference.

This is written language trying to live without oral language: surprises and shifts of focus, the expectation of another voice replying or interrupting, the emotional tone, are organized out of existence and given no equivalent on the page. There are, as Ong says, "psychological consequences" to this move: whereas pre-Ramist prose "could be richly sonorous rather than merely 'clear,' for it was the echo of a cognitive world experienced as if filled with sound and voices and speaking persons....With Ramus, the voice goes out of this world."[54] Pedagogically and in scholarly terms, those consequences continue. As Piaget refined his understanding of child language development, he gave nine- to eleven-year-olds a list of proverbs ("Drunken once will get drunk again") to match with a list of paraphrases expressing the "same ideas" ("It is difficult to break old habits"). He took any errors purely as evidence of the children's difficulty with understanding and reasoning, rather than evidence at another level of their inarticulate allegiance to language with a voice.[55] Certainly children of nine to eleven are cognitively incapable of theory, and will try to arrive at the right answers to such an exercise by imaginative guesses, but they also prefer sonority to abstraction and animation to detachment. A flat paraphrase cannot seem to them the "same idea" as a vivid and resonant phrase.

Ramism did not begin to have an influence in England till 1574, and then among schoolboys and university students rather than mature thinkers; gradually it gained popularity among Puritan preachers, and from there attained a wide influence. (The name "methodist" was later derived from Ramist sources.) Ong finds the Puritan "plain style" writers "somehow deeply distrustful of words, save perhaps in the homiletic monologue."[56] When Croll speaks of the move away from "poetry and the imagination" in science, he is tracking a pattern more sophisticated than Ramism, but one that is characterized by the same mistrust. He sees the stylistic reform of the late seventeenth and eighteenth centuries as "determined by Cartesian philosophy, or at least by the same...spirit in which the Cartesian philosophy had its origin....The sources of error, in the view of the Cartesians, are imagination and dependence upon sense impressions."[57] Ramism was part of this mix, and its tone-deafness to the imaginative and sensory qualities of both orality and literacy had a narrowing effect on thought even in the supposedly expansive Enlightenment. Francis Bacon, writing in 1605, already saw the limits of "method" in comparison to aphoristic writing:

> For first, [writing in Aphorisms] trieth the writer, whether
> he be superficial or solid: for Aphorisms, except they should
> be ridiculous, cannot be made but of the pith and heart
> of sciences; for discourse of illustration is cut off; recitals

of examples are cut off; discourse of connexion and order is cut off; descriptions of practice are cut off; so there remaineth nothing to fill the Aphorisms but some good quantity of observation: and therefore no man can suffice, nor in reason will attempt, to write aphorisms, but that he is sound and grounded. But in Methods...[the arrangement and connexion and joining of the parts has so much effect], as a man shall make a great shew of an art, which if it were disjointed would come to little. Secondly, Methods are more fit to win consent or belief, but less fit to point to action; for they carry a kind of demonstration in orb or circle, one part illuminating another, and therefore satisfy; but particulars, being dispersed, do best agree with dispersed directions. And lastly, Aphorisms, representing a knowledge broken, do invite men to enquire farther; whereas Methods, carrying a shew of the total, do secure men, as if they were at furthest.[58]

The very absence of illustrations and examples that, to the methodical, make aphorisms seem lightweight and unsubstantiated is for Bacon the virtue of the form: it forces the responsibility for synthesis back onto the writer, and tests the writer's expertise by the reader's own subsequent investigations. The temptation of "method" is to wrap everything up neatly, to present so circumscribed and finished a product that it need only be swallowed and regurgitated to count as learning. The aphorism portrays not a thought but a mind thinking, and does not complete the thought; it invites the reader to think along with it, to do further work, and not to suppose she can ever be "at furthest." As "method" superseded aphorism, curiosity was ever so slightly discouraged — and young students know how total and final a slight discouragement can be; once more it began to take on the cast, not quite of heresy, but of a minority taste.

Stanley Fish suggests that what atrophied in prose style in the late seventeenth century was a certain confusion — induced by a combination of metaphysical subject matter and syntactical ambiguity — which compelled the reader to work hard for the meaning of a passage, and whose aim was not education but transformation. Fish finds no absolute polar distinction between Ciceronian and baroque, Anglican and Puritan, or any other stylistic dichotomy that scholars of the period have proposed; rather, he distinguishes between two "experiences of reading." He calls these (inconveniently enough, since Ramus used the terms in more or less the opposite ways) the rhetorical and the dialectical, or "self-satisfying" and "self-consuming." By rhetorical he means "a language that builds its readers' confidence by building an argument they can follow"; by dialectical he means "a language that, by calling attention to the insufficiency of its own procedures, calls into question the sufficiency of the minds it unsettles" — agonistic, affectively charged, and orally grounded in its radical syntactical shifts.[59] The psychological effects of the two styles are strikingly different:

> A presentation is rhetorical if it satisfies the needs of its readers. The word "satisfies" is meant literally here; for it is characteristic of a rhetorical form to mirror and present for approval the opinions its readers already hold. It follows then that the experience of such a form will be flattering, for it tells the reader that what he has always thought about the world is true and the ways of his thinking are sufficient. This is not to say that in the course of a rhetorical experience one is never told anything unpleasant, but that whatever one is told can be placed and contained within the categories and assumptions of received systems of knowledge.
>
> A dialectical presentation, on the other hand, is disturbing, for it requires of its readers a searching and rigorous scrutiny of everything they believe in and live by. It is didactic in a special sense; it does not preach the truth, but asks that its readers discover the truth for themselves, and this discovery is often made at the expense not only of a

reader's opinions and values, but of his self-esteem. If the experience of a rhetorical form is flattering, the experience of a dialectical form is humiliating.[60]

In effect, the rational "rhetorical" voice assures the reader that all problems are soluble and that the particular problem under consideration has already been solved by the writer; the disturbing "dialectical" voice is at work on solving the problem without knowing the outcome. The rhetorical voice is collegial but emotionally distant; it can be studied and its main points marked with yellow highlighter. The dialectical voice is intimate and absorbed, taking unexpected syntactical turns, more liable to be quoted than outlined. Essentially it is private speech committed to the page. "[T]he locus of a dialectical experience is not the spoken or written word but the mind in which the word is working"[61] — in this case, *the reader's*; the point of emergence from the writer's mind is the point of entry into the reader's. The dialectical is private speech in a contagious, transmissible form.

For an illustration of the dialectical mode with a liturgical resonance, we might turn to an herbalist's charm collected in London in the 1920s — from a paraprofessional subculture oral enough to have resisted the incursions of the rhetorical:

> Here come I to cure a burnt sore.
> If the dead knew what the living endure
> The burnt sore would burn no more.[62]

Without anything resembling God-language, this has all the elements of prayer: it is a declaration of intent to solve a problem, meant for the overhearing of those who are present and not for the direct reply of those who are not. Its ambition is limited and concrete, its success absolutely contingent — on an impossibility. The dead, when they were living, *did* know what the living endure; being dead, they have forgotten. The cure will depend on other conditions so unknown as to be unnamed. The invocation of the dead lends the rhyme its potency, but acknowledges in its very structure, in its grammar and literal meaning, that the potency is lent. The very confidence generated by rhythm and rhyme incorporates the knowledge of its own collapse. The rhyme "consumes" itself by refusing to conceal that the healer has very little control over the outcome. Simplicity is the rhyme's defining strength — the monosyllables, the jigging rhythm, the emotional immediacy of compassion and intention and dread; at the same time the middle line, with its sophisticated off-rhyme *endure* and the simultaneous kindling and crushing-out of hope by that terrible *if,* casts a cold eye on "simple faith."

It is pedagogical heresy, of course, to speak against a method that "builds its readers' confidence by building an argument that they can follow." Yet liturgy is not really an argument, and self-esteem is not really its point. It is an experience, and proceeds not from point to point of logic but from state to state of consciousness. It must reach into the parts of us that exist beneath, or prior to, self-esteem, and move us as far beyond it as *King Lear* is beyond *I'm OK, You're OK.* Fish's term "self-consuming" refers both to this transformation as it evolves through the reader's encounter with a dialectical work, and to the work's exhaustion of itself in moving the reader from one state of comprehension to another:

> [A] dialectical presentation succeeds at its own expense; for by conveying those who experience it to a point where they are beyond the aid that discursive or rational forms can offer, it becomes the vehicle of its own abandonment....[T]he reader's self (or at least his inferior self) is consumed as he responds to the medicinal purging of the dialectician's art, and that art, like other medicines, is consumed in the workings of its own best effects.[63]

The thrust of the dialectical work is away from conventional reflexes — defamiliarizing; it moves the reader insistently toward perception, through freedom of language under intense physical and intellectual pressure. The dialectical work "humiliates" by forcing the confrontation with an uncontrollable reality; it recapitulates our experience of being humbled by circumstance. It accomplishes its "medicinal" purpose not by being an accurate curative dosage, but by strengthening the reader's tolerance for the uncontrollable. Even a postmodern audience, well schooled in the hermeneutics of suspicion, *still knows how to trust* when the dialectical voice speaks; this too may be a knowledge so private as to be furtive, but we can tell the difference between the voice that claims to have discovered the truth already and the voice that has to find out the truth for itself.

Paraphrase

Organization is of course indispensable for science and scholarship; facts must be established and results reproduced. But, as practiced, it is a specialized application of intellectual power that does its work by a drastic narrowing of affect. It cannot contain emotional states, only identify and analyse them — sometimes a necessary task, as in psychotherapy, but one that purposely blocks the feelings from being felt. Analytical detachment is not an end in itself; in psychotherapy it distances the patient from ungovernable emotions in order to restore them in bearable form, and in writing it views the expression critically in order to intensify its emotional power. The eighteenth century feared madness; it was more likely to mistake the "medicinal purging of the dialectician's art" for the malady than to see it as a cure. Dryden's epigram

> Great wits are sure to madness near allied,
> And thin partitions do their bounds divide[64]

(when detached from its context in the urbane and clever *Absalom and Achitophel* and used with a cautionary sense) is an uneasy

assessment of the risks of genius which, followed to its logical conclusion, would have us thicken the partitions at the expense of our
wit. Even the self-contained epigrammatism of the heroic couplet
— Pope's favorite form too — has too secure a sense of closure;
the prim rhymed pronouncement attempts to consolidate, to do-
mesticate, the idea in the form of a proverb. At worst it is a rear-
guard effort to remake literacy in the emotionally predictable mode
of orality, and one feels the loss of the unpredictable. It is at least a
coincidence worth noting that the most striking English religious
poem of the eighteenth century, Christopher Smart's *Rejoice in the
Lamb*, was the product of madness.

If, in the Reformation, contingency had seemed inescapable, in
the Enlightenment it came to seem *undesirable*: the ascendancy of
the "self-satisfying" presentation was an attempt to avoid the inchoate and the inexplicable. "No one [was] now willing," remarks Fish,
"to say, with Donne, that he intends 'to trouble the understanding,
to displace, and to discompose, and disorder the judgment.'"[65] Com-
posure was the very mark of judgment; disorder was the sign of an
imperfect understanding or a mind in darkness. Barfield observes
in a discussion of archaism in poetic diction that as grammar has
grown "more and more adapted to the concise expression of abstract
thought" it has become "less fit for the embodiment of meaning
which has not yet become abstract, and therefore eludes logical confine-
ment."[66] The idea of meaning that has not, perhaps cannot, become
abstract — meaning that exists permanently outside the confines of
logic — was an idea without a place in the eighteenth century.

Though psychohistory has its limitations as a method, it is
tempting to see the Age of Reason as the severance from consciousness of the horrors of the Reformation, and even of the states of
feeling that brought them on: an age when strong feeling itself came
to seem not only dangerous but inexplicable. "A thought to Donne
was an experience," says T. S. Eliot; "it modified his sensibility."
Thought-as-experience was a mode that the Enlightenment sought

to preclude. Eliot calls the shift of style "a dissociation of sensibility from which we have never recovered"[67]; Ian Robinson asserts that in the eighteenth century "Passion, tragedy, ecstasy, great beauty, became inexpressible in the styles of language approved by the arbiters of taste."[68] Repression at that level is an effort to avoid madness so desperate and extreme that in the long run it becomes madness. Reason itself is a sort of dissociation — at any rate a form of *detachment* from sensibility; it can be a necessary form, when sensibility is irrational in some crippling sense, but it has a cost. An artistic case in point is Nahum Tate's 1681 revision of *Lear* as a Restoration comedy, which leaves Cordelia alive and marries her off to Edgar — a consummation devoutly to be wished, no doubt, but so far from Shakespeare's intent as to be appalling and ludicrous. The sensibility that repudiated sensibility tended, in crucial ways, to become insensibility.

Rosenzweig's aversion, religious discourse conceived as "bare content" and transmittable apart from the vehicle of transmission, might never have arisen without this shift in style. George Steiner calls the eighteenth century "largely indifferent to the linguistic structures underlying literature." Its prose writers saw no necessary relation between an idea and the sounds and rhythms in which it was expressed. Its literary ideal was

> one of lucid paraphrase: the lyric or dramatic genre being an elevation, an embellishment of a content which could, in turn, be extracted from the poem and laid out in everyday prose....The work of literature was to be judged not as a linguistic artifact, defining its own stylized, extraterritorial standards of truth and relevance: it was to be seen for its explicit ethical content, and judged accordingly.[69]

The Bible itself was not off limits to this approach. Edward Harwood carried the ideal to an extreme in his 1768 *Liberal Translation of the New Testament*, which paraphrased the entire work in wreaths of Augustan eloquence. His translation was not particularly well received even in its own time — Boswell thought it "ridiculous" — but it was a logical extension of the age's preoccupation with "explicit ethical content" at the expense of form. The book has not been reprinted and is not easy to find, but Daniell quotes some tantalizing passages in *The Bible in English*:[70] Harwood's version of the phrase "Our father which art in heaven, hallowed be thy name," for example, multiplies the number of words nearly sixfold, and in the attempt to praise God in elevated style comes closer to patronizing him:

> O Thou great governor and parent of universal nature — who manifestest thy glory to the blessed inhabitants of heaven — may all thy rational creatures in all parts of thy boundless dominion be happy in the knowledge of thy existence and providence, and celebrate thy perfections in a manner most worthy thy nature and perfective of their own![71]

"Most worthy thy nature"! A squire might be congratulating a vicar on an edifying sermon. Harwood has reconstructed a prayer originally meant to illustrate directness, humility, and the refusal of public ostentation as if he were proposing a toast — and so missed the critical ethical point. He has embellished content at the expense of lucidity. Reason's indifference to the physical properties of language, its appeal to the eye and the logic rather than the ear and the mouth, cuts off the writer (and the reader and hearer) from physical sources of information; ultimately it distorts the logic by its tin ear for accurate feeling. The Prodigal Son's father, who in the King James "saw him, and had compassion, and ran, and fell on his neck, and kissed him,"[72] in Harwood

> rushed to meet him with swift and impatient steps — folded him in his arms — imprinted 1000 ardent kisses on his

lips — the tears straying down his venerable cheeks, and the big passions that struggled in his breast, choking his utterance.[73]

This is not much like Tyndale's "slightly heightened" language. Daniell points out that Harwood's dilations owe a debt to the early novels of feeling, particularly Richardson's *Pamela* and *Clarissa*; the comparison points up the difficulty with which Richardson himself and some of his contemporaries handled the language of feeling. Understatement escapes them; it is as if they cannot trust the reader to recognize feeling unless it is painted in broad strokes, in superlatives and exclamations and the sweep and swoop of uncontrollable forces. As indeed feeling may have seemed to minds that were trying to resist it. But in religious writing the method rings particularly false: "imprinted 1000 ardent kisses on his lips" seems merely *unpracticed*, unexercised feeling, to readers used to the austerity of Abraham's "God will provide the lamb, my son."[74]

When the *agon* disappears from the cultural consciousness, a kind of uncomprehending, smiling piety takes its place; religious feeling suffocates in such an air, and must be revived by artificial respiration. The devotional writing of the period is much like Harwood's in its curious mix of extravagant adjectives and happy complacency; it is puffed with an afflatus that does not belong to the Bible or the Reformation. The Methodist inspirational writer James Hervey speaks in a style positively Kaplanian in its serene self-regard:

> I have often been charmed, and awed at the sight of the nocturnal Heavens; even before I knew how to consider them in their proper circumstances of majesty and beauty. *Something* like *magic*, has struck my mind, on a transient and unthinking survey of the aethereal vault, tinged throughout with the purest azure, and decorated with innumerable starry lamps. I have felt, I know not what powerful and

aggrandizing impulse; which seemed to snatch me from the low entanglements of vanity, and prompted an ardent sigh for *sublimer objects*. Methought I heard, even from the silent spheres, a commanding call, to spurn the abject earth, and pant after unseen delights....I gaze, I ponder. I ponder, I gaze; and think ineffable things. I roll an eye of awe and admiration.[75]

It is impossible for Hervey to feel awe without being proud of his own sensitivity; reworked in our own more casual idiom, this passage could serve admirably for Reconstructionist or Unitarian or secular humanist prayer. The sense of posing in the mirror is much the same, and so is the eclipse of the essential object of contemplation by the pulse-taking concentration on one's own emotional response. Harwood and Hervey do not so much feel as try to produce appropriate feelings — which of course can only produce inappropriate ones. Even allowing for the later shift of meaning in the word "charmed" from something more like "spellbound" to something more like "delighted", there is something trivial in the airy vagueness of "I gaze, I ponder. I ponder, I gaze; and think ineffable things." Christopher Smart, who was Hervey's contemporary, takes a more minute interest in the natural realm and a more sober view of his place in it, and produces words of a quirky but much more distinctly liturgical cast:

For the names and number of animals are as the name and number of the stars.[76]

Let Achsah rejoice with the Pigeon who is an antidote to malignity and will carry a letter.[77]

For before the NATIVITY is the dead of the winter and after it the quick.[78]

For I am not without authority in my jeopardy, which I de-
rive inevitably from the glory of the name of the Lord.[79]

While Hervey watches himself have religious feelings, Smart watches the details of the natural order, and arrives at a fundamental and
hitherto unknown stability in the midst of chaos and crisis. Hervey's style pretends to be introspective, but is only self-dramatiz-
ing; Smart's style is grave and conscious of a limited miracle. Sanity
achieved beyond and in spite of madness, rather than keeping itself
anxiously this side the partition, is a surer and more comprehensive
sanity; it knows its way around the terrain, and knows the way out.

Burning bright

In fact attempts to recover sensibility were made: by Blake and
the Romantics, by the Transcendentalists, by renegade evangelicals
like Ruskin and George Eliot who brought their cadences with them
when they went from religion to unbelief. Harold Bloom observes
that the Romantics' theories of imagination "are all displaced, radical Protestant accounts of the nakedness of the soul before God."[80]
The nineteenth century, with its oscillation between excess and repression, produced its share of sensibilities that never matured, or
that disappointed in their maturity; T. S. Eliot remarks sourly that
"Keats and Shelley died, and Tennyson and Browning ruminated."[81]
But Hopkins and Dickinson wrestled with God and prevailed; like
Smart, neither was published in full till the twentieth century, and
their great wits, like Smart's and Ruskin's, were to madness near
allied, but both arrived at an absolute poetic authority in their jeopardy. The nineteenth century also introduced what Wordsworth
scholar Jonathan Bate calls "hard pastoral"[82] — what we would now
call (such are the ironies of literary terminology) Wordsworth's "un-
romanticized" vision of rural poverty, which knocked the polish off
the eighteenth century's Strephons and Chloes and prepared the way

for George Eliot's and Hardy's more sober treatments of rural life. In their uncanonical way, Smart, Blake and Wordsworth, Hopkins and Dickinson, Emerson and Ruskin and George Eliot and Hardy (and in the twentieth century Yeats) are the strongest liturgical voices after the Reformation. They had, of course, no direct influence on established liturgies. (Emerson is sometimes quoted in Unitarian and secular humanist liturgies; he was an influence on Kaplan's thought, if insufficiently on his style.) Blake, in 1790, proclaimed, "Those who restrain desire, do so because theirs is weak enough to be restrained"[83]; Ruskin, in 1860, propounded a paradox: "Until the feelings can give strength enough to the will to enable it to conquer them, they are not strong enough."[84] These two assertions — each compatible with some part of biblical sensibility — bracket a shift in the understanding of feeling.

The nineteenth century was preeminently the age of the novel; as poets struggled to revive a compromised form, novelists compounded a new one. Ong notes that the novel owes a good deal to women's practical domestic and managerial education; women were never taught in the agonistic mode, so that the tone of fiction is "more like a conversation than a platform performance."[85] Robinson claims that the novel is by nature ironic, and that its job has been to subvert the factual fixation of Enlightenment prose;[86] the social position of the great women novelists, which was itself ironic, may have had something to do with this development. Nonetheless, the extreme introspection possible to written language is a way back to a profound spoken language, even in a literary form as thoroughly domestic and conversational as the novel. Steiner finds a direct line from the Reformation's strenuous inner dialogue with God to the interiority of the novel[87]; the revelations of character and the moral effort of resolving a plot require the same rigor as non-intercessory prayer, not only for the author and the characters but for the reader.

Sensibility itself — its risks, and its permanent presence on the domestic scene — became not only a driving force in fiction, as it had been for Richardson, but a subject of fictional scrutiny. Jane Austen's *Sense and Sensibility* presents one of its errors of judgment in Marianne Dashwood's sprawling and self-indulgent nursing of a grand passion. Marianne's sister Elinor's deeper feelings, pressurized as they are by being unspeakable, are held in a restraint almost without outlet. Marianne is a disciple of Blake, while Elinor anticipates Ruskin; the younger sister cannot imagine restraining her desire, whereas the elder sends all the force of hers into the strict keeping of silence where she has no right to speak. Elinor is certainly right in maintaining a tact and self-discipline without which social relations would quickly become intolerable, and honor is worth its cost — but just barely, and one feels how much it has cost her when she can finally speak.

When the great women novelists' dialogue rises to an occasion, it is incomparable; though fictional dialogue is not real spoken language, it can reintroduce the slight heightening that conveys lived experience with force and economy. "Do you compare your conduct with his?" says Elinor, speaking to Marianne of her deceitful lover Willoughby. "No," says Marianne, "I compare it with what it ought to have been; I compare it with yours."[88] "Is it the accusations you are afraid of?" says the young heiress Catherine Arrowpoint in George Eliot's *Daniel Deronda*, declaring her love to her music teacher Herr Klesmer: "I am afraid of nothing but that we should miss the passing of our lives together."[89] This is where modern liturgists might have found their vernacular: in the anguish of secular penitence, in the decisiveness of unconventional love, in the moral effort of ordinary untheological humans to live with integrity.

But by some blindness of theological fixity, these were not the writers that modern liturgists drew from — any more than they drew from Kierkegaard, Kafka, Simone Weil or Levinas for their theological scaffolding. One of the real incongruities of history is that in liturgy the dissociation of sensibility continued, even intensified, after the two world wars. Writers whose whole object was to modernize the language of worship took virtually no notice of the agonies of modernity; instead they removed mystery and moral demand from the traditional language and introduced an air of forced celebration. They seemed to think (along with some exponents of the 1960s counterculture) that the vernacular was a language in which it was difficult to be articulate and bad form to try. It was — and is — a literate culture's misunderstanding of orality. Ong observes that "typographic folk believe that oral exchange should normally be informal [and] oral folk believe it should normally be formal"; where an oral culture does not believe in wasting its words, a literate culture has an endless supply.

> [W]here primary orality promotes spontaneity because the analytic reflectiveness implemented by writing is unavailable, secondary orality promotes spontaneity because through analytic reflection we have decided that spontaneity is a good thing. We plan our happenings carefully to be sure that they are thoroughly spontaneous.[90]

The overriding imperative of the new language was not to insult the simplicity of its supposed native speakers, the lumpenproletariat (who, however, also have an intelligence to insult, and may not care to be considered lumpen by people charged with their spiritual welfare). Paraphrase, evasion and euphemism became established techniques for rehabilitating liturgy and concealing its weaknesses. Feminism came into the mix very much as a "method" in the Ramist sense: its linguistic reforms in mainstream liturgy were moved by political logic and a dislike of existing images, not by an experience so powerful as to need an outlet in religious language. (When feminists had such experiences, they generally devised new rituals for them outside the mainstream, often in no better prose.) In the effort to spare the worshiper unpleasant thoughts, reflectiveness in oral language was treated as just another anachronism like *thee* and *thou.*

No doubt these developments arose partly from the incongruity of living with intense liturgical language — whether Hebrew, Latin, or Reformation English — in the much safer religious world of the post-World War II middle class. But safety is temporary. It is the business of liturgists to know this, and to maintain some language for danger and distress against the day when it will be needed (which, in any given life, may be *ha-yom*, today). One of the most striking things about Cranmer's phrasing is its brokenheartedness, its knowledge that danger and distress are not unlikelihoods somewhere in the indefinite future:

> The remembrance of them is grievous unto us; the burden of them is intolerable.[91]

> Patience under their sufferings, and a happy issue out of all their afflictions.[92]

> Who knowest our necessities before we ask, and our ignorance in asking.[93]

> Who knowest us to be set in the midst of so many and great dangers, that by reason of the frailty of our nature we cannot always stand upright.[94]

> We beseech thee to have compassion upon our infirmities; and those things which for our unworthiness we dare not, and for our blindness we cannot ask, vouchsafe to give us.[95]

> Increase and multiply upon us thy mercy; that, thou being our ruler and guide, we may so pass through things temporal, that we finally lose not the things eternal.[96]

Even the language of popular music — the high language of the lowly, who still insist on using high language — preserves without self-consciousness or apology the Reformation language of suffering: *For the wicked carried us away captivity / require from us a song; / How can we sing King Alfa song in a strange land?*[97] There is nothing in modern life that renders exile and sorrow irrelevant.

The point is not that Reformation language can meet all our needs — theological or emotional — or cannot be improved upon, but that it *has not* been improved upon. That no recent revisions have come near to deposing Cranmer, Coverdale, and the translators of the King James Bible (with the ghost of Tyndale in its connective tissue) as the masters of English liturgy has nothing to do with their being dead, or white, or male, or Christian, or for that matter theist; it has to do with their ability to face suffering, necessity, and the subtleties of conscience in skilled and direct language — and with the right degree of *Verfremdung* to startle, even at a distance of centuries, the mind into deeper attention. "Literature," says Steiner,

> is language, but language in a condition of special use: that condition being one of total significance, and of a significance which is — for every true poem or piece of literary prose — unique. No replacement of any semantic element, however small (consider the role of typography in Mallarmé, in e. e. cummings) will do.[98]

Steiner's definition simultaneously satisfies Staal's theory of ritual "meaninglessness" — the detail that must be preserved simply because it is always preserved — and the analogical mind's demand for meaning. Significance, in that sense, is a synthesis of content and resonance, a means of saying the necessary thing with the requisite urgency. If a change as little as "thou" to "you" or "himself" to "Godself" (and done for such worthy reasons!) destroys the whole edifice of liturgical coherence for some hearers, even for some who are in essential political agreement, it does so by calling into question the "total significance" of the whole. It is not a matter of lost faith in the conventional sense — most modern adults can handle that with some resiliency — but of lost trust. If the keepers of liturgy can so easily damage and discard the sounds of words, how carelessly will they listen to our distresses?

One can love old forms for their mortality, or fear them for their influence — feel them as powerful and fragile survivals that subtly inform our thinking, or as indomitable and inescapable presences that thwart our lives. Modern liturgy sometimes reads as if it were written by restive adolescents, resentfully tethered to their tradition and looking for ways to escape it while appearing to remain in it. Just as one needs to get far enough away from one's parents to be free of their power and admire their particular strengths, one needs a certain discretionary distance from a tradition; the faith of one's fathers must have, in one of Kaplan's happier phrases, "a vote, not a veto." But there is no lying to oneself about how much distance is necessary, and whether it is better simply to leave the tradition. Once independence is established, the full weight of responsibility in a complex world falls on both the reformer and the escapee: one's writing is judged as writing. Anyone who dismisses the old language as elitist and unnecessarily difficult has not understood the respect with which the scholarly elite of the sixteenth century — Tyndale, Coverdale, Cranmer and the rest — offered it to an uneducated public that wanted knowledge. But everyone supposed in those days that accurate understanding could save souls.

The Reformation began when the illiterate had a compelling reason to become literate. We are at a point now where much of our culture does not see a compelling reason to remain literate. This is as true in one sense of the affluent professional who reads for fun or for profit but not for moral demand as it is in another of the proverbial (and often underestimated) high school dropout who despises expurgated textbooks. The first does not want emotional literacy, whereas the second may simply never have seen it offered in books. Orality in the old sense is no longer possible, and orality in the new sense does not offer enough to replace it; spoken words do not retain their medicinal power when the airwaves dispense them as ploys and placebos. If liturgy is content to stay at that level — if it goes on earnestly attempting to reach that level — it will have mistaken its work. It must instead offer as generally as possible the means of transcendence: not simply replacing an old theological outline with a new one, but offering a way right out of the known conditions. For that, a literacy is needed that can hold uncertainty, endure doubt and shame, and arrive in the end not at security but at stamina. As at the Tower of Babel, syntax is destiny.

Chapter Four

Liturgy Terminable and Interminable

Make us glad for as many years as you have tormented us, and for the years we have seen evil.

— Ps. 90

You are the wound. You
Be the medicine.

— Robert Pinsky, "Ode to Meaning"

If modern liturgies have failed by keeping the form of Christian belief or Jewish practice while abandoning the seriousness, no one has yet suggested the opposite method: keeping the seriousness while largely abandoning the form. For the congregant inclined to seriousness (and irony), a traditional form may come to suffice, but if something must be abandoned the form is the more dispensable. It is more important to keep enforcing attention like deep harmony than it is to maintain a superficial resemblance to earlier liturgy. The 1979 Book of Common Prayer revised the *Te Deum*'s opening line, "We praise thee, O God," to the inane (and mistranslated) "You are God: we praise you."[1] How much attention can such a formula enforce, or even withstand? Would any major composer be likely to take it for a text? It conveys well enough — by accident — the modern sensibility, with its simultaneous hunger for and recoil from God: it presents the old idea as if intact, but so flattened as to make it incredible. The modern sensibility might have been better served by juxtaposing, say, Psalm 148 — "Praise the Lord from the heavens, praise him in the heights" — with Cordelia's "Nothing, my lord."[2]

The modern reluctance to praise God was not mere truculence or thanklessness — certainly not "nihilism"; it is worth thinking of Nietzsche in the same breath with Cordelia, to see what tenderness may be possible after exasperated honesty has been given its due. But praise had come to seem false, and modern liturgists could imagine no way to maintain it except by reducing it to pablum. The automatic, autonomic, movement toward praise was checked first by the consciousness that one was praising a fiction, and then by the unappeasable knowledge of the trenches, the death camps, the atomic bomb. The old pieties could not survive such a consciousness. Neither, of course, could banners and guitar music and happy assertions hope to offset it; their veneer of praise was too thin to disguise the bumps and gaps beneath. But liturgists working within established traditions where whitewashing and damage control were already standard methods could not imagine disrupting or dispensing with praise; if they could not come by it honestly, they would have to produce it dishonestly. For all their attempts at "relevance" they were missing the most salient need of all. Liturgy must work from what William James called "the recesses of feeling, the darker, blinder strata of character... the only places in the world in which we catch real fact in the making, and directly perceive...how work is actually done."[3]

Alongside the writing of prayer books, another and more important process is always going on: the remaking of language after its demolition. The child assembling language for the first time develops private speech in an atmosphere of trust; the translator enlarging the vernacular, or the writer discovering the inner life of the spoken word, trusts language to be malleable and responsive. The survivor of trauma has been to language and back; he has seen its capacities exhausted, and must nevertheless learn to use it again — or trust nothing again in his life.

The *timor mortis* that sharpened the language of the Reformation is in no sense foreign to the political and emotional breakdowns of the twentieth century. What drove many of the best minds of the modern period from the churches and synagogues was the sense that religion had no response to the world that now surrounded it. In what sense, if God is a fiction, does it matter that Jesus died for the sins of the world? In the wake of the pogroms and of Hitler and Stalin — and, in another sense, in the wake of Pol Pot — what are the Jews chosen *for*? When liturgy expresses not only an outworn cosmology but an obsolete social organization, how far can we trust its teleology or its ethics? What is it to have survived, in a sense, one's culture?

If Auschwitz and the gulags seem to the modern liturgist too far removed from the concerns of the affluent suburban congregation — or even the poor urban one — the catastrophes of family life surely are not. Secrets and forms of misery differ from family to family, but not (or not only) by socioeconomic bracket; liturgy everywhere proceeds daily in the presence of intimate suffering. Every child has experiences of shock; every adult endures thwarting and loss. What is a mother's love if a mother can sleep through one's crying? What is a mother's love if it can so fully mistake, or miss, what is in one's mind? What is a father's love if a father cannot show love, or deserts his family? What is a child's love if it declines at puberty into resentment and secrecy? What is a lover's promise if it can be broken, or a lover's faithfulness if passion or conversation cannot connect? What is a family if it breaks into hostile factions, or hangs on half-broken by drunkenness, rage or despair? What is childhood, womanhood, manhood, in the wake of brutality or sexual attack? What is it to have survived, in a sense, one's life?

Liturgy need not speak directly of any one of these things to be credible; it is seldom less credible than when it tries. But it must not lose the link between religion and extremity. Liturgy written for the mild social accommodations of congregational life has no resources for disaster; it can shed a sentimental tear, but it cannot weep. There are liturgical methods for approaching great pain, though we have not seen them competently used since the Civil Rights Movement: understatement, dignity, persistence, upheld by a searing consciousness of all that cannot be saved. In a midrash on Lamentations, God weeps at the destruction of the Temple — for which he has himself been responsible, even closing his eyes to permit the enemy's work; the chief of the angels begs him to refrain, but he will not, and commands Jeremiah: "Go call Abraham, Isaac and Jacob and Moses from their graves, for they know how to weep."[4] Modern liturgy would turn itself into a travel brochure rather than call the patriarchs from their graves; it would forfeit what is left of its authority to avoid seeing congregants weep. Yet its very evasions send some congregants into quiet emergency.

If poetry is emotion recollected in tranquillity, liturgy may be stillness maintained in turbulence: religion deals with what sets the emotions most perilously on edge. It must recreate the rawest states of mind in people who may not, at the moment, be disposed to feel them; it must trouble the hearts, even irritate the wounds, of those who come to services out of habit or in search of mild comfort. To people whose emotions are always on edge it must offer a guarantee of stability and integrity. To offer rational theological adjustments and deliberately inoffensive metaphors to suffering human beings is vastly off the point; it is, as a friend says, like using aspirin to treat a gunshot wound. Liturgy can provide no relief for the human condition if it does not understand the nature of the injury.

Repetition

Emerson, in "Self-Reliance," called prayer a disease of the will. He meant petitionary prayer — he did think there was another kind worth keeping, "the soliloquy of a beholding and jubilant soul" — and he put it at the bottom of the evolutionary ladder along with creeds, which he called a disease of the intellect. But prayer is a disease in another sense: it is repetition. In emotional distress it is the symptom that is repeated: the obsessive hand-washing or reasoning, the psychogenic pain, the self-loathing or self-starvation or self-mutilation, the catalepsy or fugue state. Emotional causes and biological triggers interact in complex ways; symptoms may be unexplainable by any event in the past, or may be markers for unspeakable fear or memory so far removed from ordinary consciousness as to be half-unknown to the sufferer. In any given case, only time and work will unravel the causes. Prayer too may be a symptom: an obscure code (symbolic? "meaningless"?) that demands to be repeated whether the worshipers understand it or not. Even when it is not asking for something — or not with the literal expectation of being answered — it returns again and again to a set form. It may be a biological compulsion; it may be the one expressible manifestation of some obscure and appalling trauma.

Survivors of the Nazi camps speak of the eclipse of language that lives just below consciousness for the rest of their lives, the impossibility of conveying to anyone who did not suffer it the nature of the experience. Soldiers often say nothing of the real nature of war when they come home. Certain childhood experiences outstrip the ability of language to develop: shocks of fear, pains prolonged or repeated, emotional contradictions, coercion or violence or abandonment. At their most confounding, these are the experiences that may stop a child speaking altogether for a time, like Maya Angelou at the age of eight after rape.[5] Piaget noted children's difficulties with repeating even the plot of a myth or a fairy tale in the right order with all the elements present;[6] it is exponentially more difficult to assemble straight from one's lived experience the narrative of a terrible event one did not understand. Elaine Scarry notes the difficulty even for medically trained adults of finding words to describe pain: "Physical pain does not simply resist language but actively destroys it, bringing about an immediate reversion to a state anterior to language, to the sounds and cries a human being makes before language is learned."[7] When pain is compounded by confusion, humiliation, and in some cases a sense of complicity, the event remains conceptually intractable as well.

For a child the cognitive problem is so overwhelming that the experience may be assigned to a place in the consciousness whose only task is to guard it. But the adult must find words or go on reenacting the trauma. The transformation of unspoken experience into physical symptoms — whose severity may be socially crippling, or lethal — is a function of the wordlessness of pain; the symptom reaches back to the annihilation of language as to the sole source of its understanding. Peter Shabad suggests that repetition is a means of ensuring that the experience will not be forgotten: symptoms arise in the absence of anyone else who comprehends the experience, as "memorials to one's lonely suffering." Had a witness been present immediately after the event, repetition would never have become necessary; failing a witness, one's body becomes the witness.

> Perhaps it is this very transformation of experienced suffering into a witnessed reality at the moment it occurs that inoculates experience against traumatization....[I]f trauma can be known only "after the fact" through its residual trail of post-traumatic communication, it suggests that being alone and not being able to convey one's experience immediately are intrinsic to the transformation of suffering into trauma....[A] person may need a sense of connectedness in order to have the freedom to feel.[8]

But the connectedness must be genuine, and the witness a trusted receiver of the story. Even in short-term therapy immediately following the event, whose whole object is to keep suffering from developing into trauma, an impersonal or canned approach may not reach far enough and may be resented.[9] For those who have lived a long time without speaking of their experience, the process of assimilating it into full consciousness is not a quick one. The therapist must become a trustable witness, and the possibility of telling the story must become imaginable. Shabad emphasizes the need for the consent of the whole personality to the shift: "When therapeutic movement comes too quickly, patients are tempted to break a silent loyalty oath they took with themselves during the loneliest of times, an oath never to forget."

> [I]f these patients' symptoms were to be killed off, the story that they contain would not be told, and the patients' experiences of suffering, starved of a life-giving witness, would shrivel up into the meaninglessness of a hallucinatory episode. Symptoms thus are pregnant with constructive meaning, constructed as they are with the purpose of bringing the dignity of recognition, sometimes many years later, to a person's experiences of lonely suffering. As those experiences finally are revealed in the presence of a credibly empathetic witness, they are infused with the meaningful breath of having real life.[10]

Neurochemistry has begun to make sense of the wordlessness of trauma. The brain *in extremis*, it appears, handles memory differently than in ordinary times. In general, the presence of an event in the memory is directly correlated with its emotional weight: a powerful event, like a powerful sentence, is powerfully memorable. Adequate words may be elusive, but more likely because of the event's uncompromising, crystalline specificity than its vagueness. But an event of overwhelming violence may, more or less literally, shatter the memory:

> If the emotional arousal is too high, the hippocampus [a structure that works with the amygdala in the organization of all conscious memories] is hindered in making a proper categorization and evaluation of the traumatic event. What

happens, chemically, is that a traumatic experience or painful memory...causes the level of cortisol in the brain to rise.
Cortisol, the stress hormone, works by binding to receptor
sites in the hippocampus, but when emotion gets too high
too much cortisol binds to each neuron. The onslaught increases the metabolism of the cells so much that they essentially overheat and die. As a result, the hippocampus can't
organize the components of the traumatic experience into a
unified whole. The person can only reexperience the painful sensory fragments, not the event. The traumatic experience is recorded as separate and dissociated from other life
experiences, and takes on a timeless and alien quality.[11]

Symptoms arise as the brain's effort to comprehend the experience
fails and is reattempted. "A traumatized individual is often unable to
formulate a unified conception of the harrowing experience, yet con-
tinues to be haunted by the powerful emotions of the experience in
the form of fragmented sensory perceptions and emotional states."[12]
The disorientation — which may give rise to flashbacks, breaks in
time, or competing organizations of personality — neither wears off
nor becomes tolerable; the traumatized person lives in a half-light of
alienated knowledge, the permanent state of *Verfremdung* entailed
in survival.

The extraordinary thing about human psychosomatic functioning is that *language* provides the release. In spite of our cultural familiarity with passwords and spells, transformative priestly formulas, and a biblical God identified with the Word, we do not think
of words as having power to subdue the manifestations of madness.
Nevertheless, finding words for an inner disaster makes it by slow
degrees less disastrous. The event is taken up into the shape of the
sufferer's life, given a context and a significance. The repetition compulsion goes on repeating itself until language provides an outlet,
whereupon physical and behavioral symptoms can resolve themselves
and disappear: words are the resolution. Recent neurochemistry has

discovered that the retraining of neurons in any learning process is assisted by speech; the very neural map of one's language apparently changes as one becomes more articulate.[13] In the exacting task of teaching oneself sanity, the map of one's whole being must be redrawn. It is remarkable that the nineteenth century, one of the most mechanistic periods of scientific discovery — indeed the very years of the nineteenth century that saw the discovery of certain material causes of disease, the rise of microbiology, sterilization, the germ theory — should so accurately have observed the internal workings of the psyche, whose material basis could not be understood by the science of the time. The "talking cure" would seem to be the least intuitive treatment for physical symptoms caused by physical events of the past — except that, empirically, it works.

Vygotsky and Ong, from their two distinct disciplines, say that writing restructures consciousness. Psychotherapy restructures consciousness through a speech as rigorous as the most demanding writing. The cooperative work between thought and feeling (the analytical powers of the frontal cortex and the emotional capacities of the limbic system) that is generally done in childhood and youth, as we learn to control our impulses, is done painstakingly between patient and therapist against the established habits of a difficult life. Scarry speaks of the miraculous quality of speech recovered after its eclipse by pain: "to be present when a person moves up out of that pre-language and projects the facts of sentience into speech is almost to have been permitted to be present at the birth of language itself."[14] The *psych-* in psychology is not an accident or a mistake: the repair of the personality is the repair of the soul. Articulation, the evolution of a coherent narrative from a set of fragmented memories (as a writer might work from a disjointed set of notes): therapeutic speech catches not the idea but the personality at the point of emergence. To tell the story of one's pain is to organize mental chaos into comprehensible form — a process, as Mark Johnson suggests of the organization of a life story, that by nature involves moral thinking.

The writer must work without a witness, writing for the imagined presence of a reader whose trust can be won. For the patient, the presence of a trusted therapist witnesses the words into being and the mind into coherence.

If the private language of the therapy session can restructure consciousness through speech, how should the public language of liturgy attempt any less? Considering that psychotherapy is preeminently a means to work through disorders of feeling — a means whereby, in a relationship of utmost privacy, an emotionally wounded person finds words for the wound — a therapeutic age should hold liturgy to a high standard. Though liturgy cannot reproduce the acute mutual responsiveness of the therapeutic relationship, something of what is done in private between patient and therapist is done in public by congregation and prayer book — by the sheer reliability of daily and weekly services, by the liturgy's probing of the conscience, by the narrative implied as the story of the people illuminates or collides with the story of the worshiper, by the relationship implied between intelligence and strong feeling in the structure of the ritual. In the absence of a witness — and liturgy reaches people who may be unable to pay a therapist, and who may be friendless — the collective monologue becomes a collective witness; the imagined presence of God gives words a way into the soul.

Contemporary liturgists often assume that repetition is mere tedium, and introduce novelties; most of these try not to produce any difficult states of mind, and restructure consciousness downward if at all. Congregations are liable to become attached to the novelties anyway and subject them to a repetition that their quality will not bear, simply because repetition is a compulsion; the need to trust is so great that it will attach itself to any available object. For the sufferer, the persistent disappointment of being offered greeting-card sentiment in place of recognition becomes a bitter frustration — and for most people it is not a frustration with the writing but with themselves: they trust the liturgist to know how to provide recognition, and blame themselves for not knowing how to receive it.

When liturgists do attempt to address violence and trauma — and to "raise" consciousness directly — the vocabulary they use often attaches itself too firmly to the terminology of the moment and lends itself to special occasions rather than to repetition. They miss the opportunity to introduce the thought more subtly into the core of the liturgy, where it might surprise a victim or a perpetrator unawares and work a more genuine change. An example that approaches the problem fairly gracefully is Thomas H. Troeger's "Holy and Good is the Gift of Desire," written (in partnership with composer Carol Doran) to accompany a sermon on male violence against women. The hymn addresses with unusual candor the goodness of the body in Christian tradition and the crippling of trust by domestic violence and rape, though with a slight edge of the documentary:

Refrain: Holy and good is the gift of desire.
God made our bodies for passion and fire,
Intending that love would draw from the flame
Lives that would shine with God's image and name.

God weeps for all people abandoned, abused.
God weeps for the women whose bodies are bruised.
God weeps when the flame that God has infused
is turned from its purpose and brutally used.

God calls to the women, God calls to the men:
"Don't hide from the terror or terror will win.
I made you for love, but love must begin
by facing the violence without and within."

God knows that our violence is mixed with our dust:
God's son was a victim of violence and lust,

> for Jesus revealed that women will trust
> a man who in action is tender and just.[15]

This is literate, serviceable verse in the Protestant hymn tradition; the AAAA rhyme scheme is not easy to carry off well, and the avoidance of pronouns for God (as mandated by the inclusive-language checklist) is unobtrusively handled except in the third line of the first stanza. The words are sober and earnest in their sympathy, though they arise more from sympathy than from a sense of experienced truth. The real dissonance arises in the last stanza, where sympathy collides with the liturgical imperative of all Protestant hymns to anchor their message in New Testament imagery. From a fairly well-tuned mixture of modern and biblical language in the first two lines of the stanza, the last two seem rather suddenly to consolidate the position of Jesus as feminist ally; the syntax turns on a "for" whose function is wholly unclear (was *that* why they crucified him?). The phrase "a man who in action is tender and just" may do something to restructure the consciousness, or affirm the achieved character, of men who sing it, but there is something unsatisfactory about offering either for men's emulation or for women's hopes of recovery a man who could carry on a conversation with a woman but who was no woman's husband or lover. It is hard not to see this invocation of Jesus as (the gentlest and most generously intended) theological opportunism; it is not quite possible to imagine the hymn in general and lasting use.

Just as a therapist who is more attached to a methodology than to the patient's own words will eventually exhaust the patient's trust, a liturgy that gives the slightest suggestion of having an axe to grind will alert the congregant's suspicions; even when it is more or less the congregant's own axe, its edge will be tested exactingly. (Is a feminine image feminist enough? is it suitable for its context? does it read like an afterthought or a sop? does it rise to the level of the surrounding passage, or failing that drag the whole passage down to its level?) When it is not the congregant's own axe, it may fail immediately; for example, men or boys who have suffered domestic violence or sexual assault — and their feminist allies — may feel that Troeger has acquired only a partial understanding of the problem. In another sense, the essential axe-grinding nature of evangelical Christianity (and of the New Testament itself) is a given for its consenting participants, and provides an inexhaustible range of biblical allusions. Troeger's use of these is often incisive, especially when he takes a circuitous approach; in one hymn he begins with Cain's rage and Abel's blood crying from the ground to build gradually a powerful protest against war.[16] Allusions must be handled with respect — they must provide real illumination, not give a sense of being merely dragged in to bolster an opinion — but when they work well, they add an unshakeable authority.

Allusiveness is in fact what takes the place of person-to-person intimacy in liturgy: a shared body of stories and phrases and images, whose familiarity parallels the accumulated material of therapy as a ready store of mutual understanding. Jewish and Christian liturgy is a tissue of quotes from the Bible — not only long passages like the Psalms and the weekly readings, but short phrases woven into the prayers. It is possible to imagine a modern liturgy that draws not only on these sources but on literature and science for its allusions; it would have to be done with extraordinary skill not to appear a ridiculous patchwork, but it might bridge the gap between religious and secular sensibilities. The "talking cure" is built on moments of recognition; between patient and therapist no source of recognition is off limits, and between liturgist and congregation perhaps the same should be true. If words can restructure consciousness, words meant for repetition must offer each time the pattern of the restructuring: not theory but practice.

The Language of Rocks

The emotions available to us depend more heavily than we suppose on the words available for them. As Anna Wierzbicka has noted, the German *Gefühl* makes no distinction between physical and emotional feelings;[17] particular shadings of anger differ between Polish and English, and in Polish it is impossible to say one is angry at God;[18] the Tahitian language has no concept of sadness, and has other words for depressed states which cannot be rendered in English.[19] *Angst* has a specific enough shade of meaning to have entered English untranslated,[20] and to judge by recent academic usage *jouissance* is well on the way. Having a concept like *Schadenfreude* available in one's language enables an evaluative look at glee in another's fall; whether it skews the odds away from or toward having the emotion might not be easy to determine, though so many English-speaking writers have adopted the word that it seems at least to have been a phenomenon waiting for a descriptor. *Ḥesed* has greater speed and immediacy than "lovingkindness": in the Hebrew usage it suggests not a caressing beneficence but an alertness of perception, an alacrity of response. What is true of a foreign language is equally true of different registers in one's own; a shift of register can provide words for states we have dimly sensed but never fully experienced till the words made it possible. "I am sorry for't," says Shakespeare's Paulina: "All faults I make, when I shall come to know them, / I do repent."[21] "Because your merit cries out upon myself, I have been trying to do it away," says Marianne Dashwood to Elinor.[22] To know that one is likely not only to have faults, but to need them pointed out — to learn for the first time that one has been systematically and thoroughly wrong: these shifts of perception come to us by example, the fictional character's experience glossing one's own.

Psychological language has two emotional vocabularies, one for the therapist and one for the patient; perhaps no other field is so strikingly polarized between the most distant and the most intimate.

It achieves full dissociation of sensibility when psychologists talk to each other: the field whose job is emotion is full of affectless words for emotional states. From the specialized coinages of classical Freudian terminology to the buzzwords of popular psychology — *transference, cathexis, dysfunctional, acting out, venting, assertiveness, negativity* — the analytical vocabulary is meant to ensure detachment and to keep empathy well within bounds. (A few clinical terms do enter the vernacular with enthusiasm; young people have embraced the opportunity to describe teachers or bosses or sergeants as "anal.") Professional terminology does help professionals do their work without breaking down — and helps to distinguish them from the patients — but has limited use in the therapy session. Between patient and therapist, "the charge of affective meaning is the currency of exchange."[23]

A significant number of psychologists have written on metaphorical language as a therapeutic phenomenon — not so much a tool, which would presuppose its predictable use, but an indicator of the depth and successful progress of the therapy. As an associative process, metaphor helps in the assembling of a story from the scattered pieces of a life; often it is the most accurate language for describing states of mind to a trusted witness. By nature, "the language of inner experience and self-discovery is largely metaphorical;"[24] the right metaphor deployed at the right moment is "so starkly self-evident that explanations are superfluous."[25] Between therapist and patient, metaphor arises intuitively with no particular conscious effort or training. In good therapeutic relationships, "sustained bursts of novel figurative language"[26] tend to evolve collaboratively at points of particular insight and are integral to the therapy; in less successful relationships the therapist is more likely to impose a metaphor over the patient's overt or covert objections as an insight the patient must be brought to accept.[27] The most striking language, arrived at collaboratively, arrests the attention and causes a permanent shift of perception: "a truly novel metaphor is not so likely to be incorporated into the ongoing hum of the personality, but rather alters the tonal structure itself."[28]

Murray Cox and Alice Theilgaard have explored this process with particular intelligence and subtlety. They call their therapeutic approach the "Aeolian Mode" — a term that for some readers may have unpleasantly vague and lyrical overtones, but which refers, precisely enough, to the Aeolian harp's instantaneous response to the movement of the surrounding air. The therapist's associative responses to the patient's words may strike with the same quick sensitivity as the pendant weights on the harpstrings; they may come as lines of verse or other literary allusions whose metaphors can be given back (sometimes in mutated form) to the patient. The point is not so much for the therapist to quote the lines directly, which could become a tiresome exercise in erudition, as to let their emotional power provide associations to take the patient to another level. The delicacy of the process is striking; the authors speak of the deep reflectiveness into which some patients fall at a chance word, even when the therapist has merely followed a hunch.

Many of Cox and Theilgaard's examples are drawn from their therapy groups in a hospital for psychotic criminal offenders, so this is not light work; in one instance, when a patient convicted of multiple stabbings spoke of having shoplifted perfume, Cox thought of Lady Macbeth — "There's the smell of the blood still" — and gently inquired after the group session whether the smell of blood had ever "concerned" the patient when she relived the stabbing incidents. She replied with an extraordinary disclosure:

> "The smell of blood? No, not theirs. But there *was* a smell of my own [from a cut received during a struggle]. I couldn't get away from it. It smelt as though you hadn't washed for months. It was a dirty smell; especially when it was dry. The police got me away from [the scene of the crime] quickly — *but I couldn't get away from my own blood.*"[29]

In this case Lady Macbeth is no mere figurehead of the literary canon, but more or less an archetype of indelible guilt. Another group of patients — described as all having "taken major risks of one sort or another with their own lives, or the lives of their victims" — when offered a metaphor without a literary source, "I wonder who would win the gold medal for skating on thin ice?", rushed to respond with their stories, at considerable risk to their own and each other's equanimity. The authors recognize that the metaphor permitted a window of safety by being merely a notion and not a command: "It invited and it did not threaten. It evoked and it did not invade."[30]

Archaic language — as the patients themselves define it, which is not necessarily language out of old books but may simply be language of particular force and feeling — is not an obstacle or an irrelevancy to the therapeutic process: it arises, as in students' writing, at heightened moments. Cox and Theilgaard specifically note the language of Shakespeare and the King James Bible as still alive, and their patients as responsive to it; one of their groups actually discussed the difference between "entreat me not to leave thee" (Tyndale, via the King James) and "do not urge me to go back and desert you" (the New English Bible) in two translations of Ruth 1:16, and preferred the spareness and emotional presence of the first.[31] They valued old language precisely for its remoteness, and for its ability to get beneath their defenses: "It's a legacy....It's how we used to think when we were very alone; when we were trees; and when we were rocks." "[T]hese things...original things...may be the 'from' that everything comes from. The unconscious is more real; it's more enduring; and it has endured me."[32] "The archaic and poetic is 'what else there is.' It hints at things....It is far away. It hangs about a bit. It lingers. It's got a stillness around it." "It takes you back further than your own early life."[33] "It doesn't mean more but it's more readily understood."[34] These are not the reactions modern liturgists expect from their congregations. In the effort to spare the worshipers difficulty, they often systematically deprive them of language that is not so much difficult as surrounded by a "stillness" that they assume to be no longer comprehensible. Cox and Theilgaard quote Stephen Prickett's *Words and* The Word: *Language, Poetics and Biblical Interpretation* to emphasize that early modern English is

> still present to us as a current linguistic idiom; *in use* every day in churches and theatres, taught and discussed in schools, seminaries, and universities, broadcast in some form almost every day on radio and television. It is not the language of ordinary colloquial speech, but then, *it never was.*[35]

The old biblical language was always meant to provide that air of something beyond the known, or something known long ago, that inwardly confirms the possibility of a witness. If the dead knew what the living endure — which maybe, in this sense, they do — old language is their signature, their echo.

Prickett emphasizes the international character of early modern English (which is equally current in Britain, North America and the English-speaking Caribbean, Australia and New Zealand, and English-speaking Africa and Asia). Its scope for ambiguity, still easily handled by readers of all classes, refutes the assumption of modern biblical translators that "present-day English represents a popular scientific and materialist culture, ill-at-ease with ambiguities or mystery."[36] Prickett is particularly struck by a comment by John Bois, secretary of the King James committee: "We have not thought that the indefinite sense ought to be defined."[37] Such reticence, Prickett points out, shows a regard for the complexities of text and reader uncommon among recent biblical translators, who seem (except for the literary translators) not to have asked themselves,

> How far is it possible, in the words of the *Good News Bible*'s Preface, "to use language that is natural, clear, simple, and unambiguous," when the Bible is *not about* things that are natural, clear, simple, and unambiguous?[38]

Cox and Theilgaard's patients — no ivory-tower theorizers — insist on the ambiguities.

Poets are sometimes heard to say that poetry saves lives. In their understanding, a poem supplies certain valid equivalents of physical affection, and heals certain emotional injuries, *purely through language.* Biblical and liturgical language once did so too, and might still, if liturgists and translators wished. But everything depends on the writer's being, in the deepest sense, committed to memory; only words written in that state can themselves be remembered. Entreaty is different from urging; not only the plaintive assonances between "entreat me" and "leave thee," but also the subliminal sense of reversal, as if Ruth were saying "*I* entreat *thee*," give the passage its tenderness. To work deliberately against such resonances is to enforce a profound physical forgetting. Steiner, in "The Distribution of Discourse," decries the steep decline of memorization in modern education as "planned amnesia;"[39] when religion abandons language that can be memorized it takes part in the same cultural erasure. To read Steiner's indictment with some knowledge of traumatic amnesia is particularly painful; there seems no reason to encourage any deliberate kind.

False Witness

The emotions available to us depend not only on the culture's vocabulary but on its sense of the common human capacities and limits. We may grow up with the expectation that valentines and Mother's Day cards must be given, anniversaries remembered and expensive dates recompensed, on pain of reprisal; that jealousy can, and should, reach operatic pitch on the slightest pretext; that consolation depends on a generous measure of flattery; that the emotional rhythms of daily life hang on offenses, imagined slights, revenges and punishments, threats and manipulations. Or we may grow up believing that the fragility of the lives entrusted to our love should overrule unfounded suspicion and grievance; that other people are likely to have many preoccupations besides oneself; that there is a certain consolation even in painful truth, and that honor has something more to do with integrity than repute. The emotional range of the first pattern looks wider at first glance, but is monotonous and relentless; the second, with its subtle and responsive adjustments, can quietly achieve wonders. There are similar patterns in the religious realm: there is religion that defends its formulas against questioning, is always on the watch for defectors and heretics, and believes God can be insulted, and religion that studies humaneness, arrives at its formulas through the questions of a broken heart, and will not trade on God's favor. The emotions — and the actions — available to one mode would never occur to the other: the very patterns of consciousness have developed along different lines.

In a sense the first pattern presupposes trauma — and the compulsive reproduction of trauma — as the unvarying ground of social and family life. The second knows the perpetual risk of trauma, and its forbearance and generosity are strict precautions against reproducing it. Liturgy, thus far, has often mixed the two modes indiscriminately. It has alternated between what Andrew Shanks calls the "pathos of glory" — bald triumphalism, the assertion that one's religion is always right — and the "pathos of shakenness," the capacity for accurate self-assessment and repentance.[40] (The repentance has nearly always been individual and the triumphalism collective.) In Shanks's view the duty of liturgy is not to prop up established structures and habits of belief but to serve as "a medicine against propaganda:"[41] to undermine certainty, to build in self-questioning, and to convey an experience of the sublime which is "at the same time both *aesthetically compelling* and yet also, in some way or another, *difficult to grasp.*"[42] The similarity of this language to Shklovsky's is striking; Shklovsky might have said that the pathos of shakenness uses a language structurally different from the pathos of glory. Where the language of shakenness prolongs the perception — "because the process of perception is an aesthetic end in itself and must be pro-longed" — the language of the pathos of glory short-circuits it: the idea at the point of emergence is ambushed by complacency even as it appears.

Shanks derives his terms from what Julien Benda, in *La trahison des clercs*, calls simply "pathos": the popular craving for the grand emotional sweep of propaganda, "the desire to be morally horrified, alarmed, filled with righteous indignation and scorn, for the sake of the pleasurable stimulus this provides; and so to have the further de-licious thrill of feeling summoned to heroism."[43] For Benda the anti-dote to this state of excitability is "ease," reason, equanimity, a total and principled abstinence from fervor. Shanks finds the matter more complicated. For one thing, Benda expends considerable emotional energy on despising popular emotion; it is impossible even for him to react to intellectual dishonesty with "ease" when its consequences may be so dire. To stand up to the inflamed emotions of outraged complacency, Shanks concludes, it is not enough to renounce in-tense emotion; one needs the counterweight of an intense *inward* emotion to resist the pull of the outward. This inward emotion is bound up with moral judgment. A refined aesthetic education, as Germany eventually found, may have severe moral limitations if it centers on *Gefühl* for its own sake; feeling that merely seeks to be-come more intensified will not be particular about the means. But feeling subjected to severer refinements becomes something more than emotional transport. The "pathos of shakenness" is an ago-nized questioning of received ideas, "a registering of the sheer inten-sity of moral chiaroscuro belonging to any really decisive moment of truth."[44] It is a confrontation between feeling and thought in which neither defeats the other.

For Shanks the pathos of shakenness is always on the side of the ill-used and the disenfranchised; what it is shaken *by* is the sheer misery of the body left unprotected. But it refuses to oppose "main-stream establishment dogma" with "the even more regimented counter-dogma of a sectarian, or revolutionary, counter-establishment."[45] Propaganda and the pleasurable stimulus of righteous indignation are known to countercultures as well as establishments; any veteran of leftist or rightist radical politics knows the thrill of abandoning moral scruple *because* one is disenfranchised. The oppressed identity group can exert as illegitimate a pressure, especially on its own members, as the oppressor. What Milan Kundera characterized as the "two tears" of kitsch — the first tear of genuine emotion and the second tear of self-congratulation for having had the emotion, "together with all mankind"[46] — flow with remarkable ease for any group that thinks it has the right answer.

The relation between aesthetics and ethics, so often characterized as opposition, thus turns out to be something more unstable and less predictable. For Kundera, kitsch is the common denominator of all totalitarian systems; we may see Nazi spectacle, socialist-realist art, and (by extension) feminist double-axe jewelry and porcelain figurines of big-eyed children in uniform as visual manifestations of the same demand for unquestioning loyalty. For Shanks, "shaken" art is a refusal to override allegiance to the truth with allegiance to a group or an ideology.

Opinions vary on the date of emergence of anything that could be called kitsch; the nineteenth century gets some votes as the point when mass production became possible. The eighteenth might give it competition as the point when sentimentality became possible. (Shanks locates the origins of the pathos of shakenness in the late eighteenth century, as poets like Blake and Hölderlin attempted "ventures of chastened reconstruction" after the Enlightenment's "arid reductionism."[47]) But the problem may go back much further. Moses, we may assume, would not have thought mass production a necessary condition for false production. To the skeptical reader it is not immediately clear why the golden calf, or Psalm 115's idols that have "mouths, but they speak not; noses, but they smell not; feet, but they walk not," are any more false than a God whose mouth and nose and feet are not there at all, or exist as verbal rather than visual metaphor. The answer seems to have to do with a certain austerity of feeling: the idol can be comfortably affirmed, whereas the God of Abraham, Isaac and Jacob is preeminently the God of discomfort. For the prophets, God's incorporeality is bound up with his inexorable moral demand; idols do not insist upon justice. No doubt the prophets would be disturbed by later generations' domestication of the invisible God and their softening of his moral demand. As Richard A. Cohen observes in an essay on Levinas, there is a difference between *ehyeh asher ehyeh* ("I will be what I will be") and *che sera sera* ("What will be will be").[48] The enigma of the first declaration, understood in its full uncanniness, ignites moral effort; the fatalism of the second subsides into resignation.

The question of kitsch may look initially like a pair of callipers to measure whether your brow is high, low or middle. But what kitsch does to art and to liturgy is a function of what it does, or fails to do, to consciousness. The kitsch image or idea — flag, kitten, angel, slogan — is a schematic rendering of reality, reassuring because one knows how to feel about it; it triggers emotional recognition and demands no intellectual work. It promises at first glance to evoke no feeling needing further resolution. People who prefer kitsch feel intimidated or put in the wrong by the work of comprehending art; they find it difficult to comprehend the latitude, and the limits, of personal interpretation. They are not at home with analogical exploration, which provides no right answers (while still insisting that some analogies are more plausible than others). Kitsch comforts them by assuring them that they do not have to know their way around history, art history, metaphor, or the range of their own minds.[49]

Thus what kitsch does politically it has first done psychologically. By inhibiting the associative process, it serves as an intellectual and moral (and even emotional) shortcut. People who prefer kitsch feel they should not have to confront disturbance; the resulting pious animus against people and ideas that disturb can be lethal. In Kundera's definition, kitsch "excludes everything from its purview which is essentially unacceptable in human existence"; it represents "the absolute denial of shit,"[50] functions as "a folding screen set up to curtain off death."[51] Anyone who brings up the unacceptable partakes in its unacceptability, and becomes — in effect and sometimes in fact — the natural target of a totalitarian system, whose aim is to eradicate the unacceptable. "When the heart speaks, the mind finds it indecent to object. In the realm of kitsch, the dictatorship of the heart reigns supreme."[52] The speech of the heart, which sounds so gentle and harmless, shades effortlessly into the hardening of the heart.

To the person who sees its inadequacy, kitsch is not a consolation but a threat. It conveys a *false* sense of security, known in advance to be false: the kitten never has fleas or coughs up a hairball, the big-eyed child never whines. The amygdala, in search of emotional weight, is presented with weightless emotion: the "unbearable lightness" that sees the past only with nostalgia and the future only with optimism. By compelling an emotional response, but standardizing the emotion and giving it no access to thought, kitsch pretends to be a witness but is not. It presents a static symbol in place of the intimate regard of a consciousness equal to or greater than one's own. A friend who has watched this book develop — and who defends kitsch, up to a point, as a means of forcibly inducing feeling in the alienated consciousness — nevertheless sees the limitations of kitsch in doing anything further with the consciousness once it is re-engaged:

> Kitsch is unilayered execution of an idea, one-dimensional, so that regardless of the complexity of the idea, the work defies cognitive expansion or subsurface experience....[A]fter the initial emotional reaction, the observer is forcibly barred from any further interaction. We dislike kitsch because we feel betrayed by the implied artistic promise of further engagement,

and are instead intentionally and overtly excluded from any
deeper connection....Art meets you where you are and draws
you further; kitsch meets you where you are and smiles.[53]

Even an infant can tell the difference between the smile that invites
it to play and the smile that displays to the grownups how much
Auntie loves little babies. Kitsch can return the alienated consciousness to feeling — the first tear; but it cheats feeling by denying it
further associative linkages — the premature resolution of the second tear. Kitsch may be the mind's way of supplying a substitute
witness when none is available — a cartoon image of a witness, with
exaggerated attributes, because the subtler and quirkier smile of the
real witness cannot be imagined beforehand — but essentially it is a
fatalist form. It is not interested in what happens next.

Outside the therapeutic setting, it is possible that the dissociative
trance of flight from one's suffering can be matched and mastered only
by the *associative* trance of work. Scarry speaks of work as the externalization of pain: "the wholly passive and acute suffering of physical
pain becomes the self-regulated and modest suffering of work. Work
is, then, a diminution of pain: the *aversive intensity* of pain becomes
in work *controlled discomfort.*"[54] Artistic work, starting as it does from
a need felt by no one but the artist, is a particularly compulsive form
of externalization. It seldom occurs to anyone but the artist to think
of the practice of art as a cure for suffering — which is why art is
considered a "frill" in public education: it appears to be too much fun
for the artist and too much a cultural chore for the audience to have
anything to do with cure. The uncritical forms of art therapy and
music therapy and "journaling" have some credibility as behavioral
modifiers, but neither our therapeutic nor our educational system
has grasped how much more therapeutic highly critical and highly
disciplined art is — not because it builds character, or perpetuates
cultural literacy, or provides an outlet for creativity, or toughens the

emotional hide through constructive criticism, but because it offers something more preoccupying than one's own pain.

In any art practiced at full strength, *the repetition of culture overrides the repetition of trauma by educating the emotions.* The necessary combination of motor skill, analytical rigor and emotional concentration enlists and reorients the whole personality. The artist, even when working alone, is taken out of isolation and set in a cultural lineage of the living and the dead as a practitioner who can be judged. Whereas the kitsch image has no significant relationship to an artistic lineage — even its realism is merely functional, allowing the image to be instantly recognized — art emulates or quarrels with earlier art, and that lineage is an integral part of the artist's self-definition and self-assessment. The distinction between "high" and "low" art is more or less immaterial: steady practice in whatever cultural idiom will override suffering simply by being a discipline. But when practice entails not only facility but full emotional presence — when one is required, on cue and for the sake of the work, to comprehend and to reproduce a strong feeling — the discipline goes beyond skill. The task has moral importance: you must do it right for its own sake, and make whatever accommodations you have to make in your emotional life in order to do it right. At this level of demand, art runs parallel to biological reproduction; the work ceases to be in any sense "*self*-expression" and becomes expression — extrusion — of the other. The process of working creates the work, and the work creates the audience (both in the sense of capturing their attention and of reconfiguring their minds). One's own character is imprinted in some unpredictable way on the work as it is on the child, but as with the child one does not have complete control over the process and it is not the point of the work. The imprinting is also reciprocal, the work leaving its signature on the artist as the child does on the parent. In whatever cultural idiom — and in the hands of the right performer, profundities can arise in surprising places — art changes both the maker and the recipient.

Liturgy is "performative" in a different sense from art — the worshiper is not rehearsing a piece for presentation to an audience but enacting each time the community's relationship to an invisible hearer — but the result is similar: a self purged of self-indulgence. One's needs are met indirectly, through meeting the fixed requirements of the ritual. Modern liturgy, with its carefully engineered spontaneities, thwarts this indirection and makes self-indulgence a central aim of group worship. The unrevised free-verse prayer, the extempore discussion after the sermon, the psychodrama-style enactment of the weekly biblical reading, do not quite evoke the established kitsch emblems of the pathos of glory, but they give us the false smile of acceptance that is really the refusal to witness. Spontaneity in most people, when it is required to appear in a group of strangers, is next kin to stereotype; it will not present the most private and pressing dismays, which must be protected from the casual gaze of the group, but searches for something acceptable to say. Director Peter Brook's trenchant remarks on the disappointments of method acting are relevant here:

> [I]n basing his gestures on his observation or on his own spontaneity the actor is not drawing on any deep creativity. He is reaching inside himself for an alphabet that is also fossilized, for the language of signs from life that he knows is the language not of invention but of his conditioning…. What he thinks to be spontaneous is filtered and monitored many times over. Were Pavlov's dog improvising, he would still salivate when the bell rang, but he would feel sure it was all his own doing. "I'm dribbling," he would say, proud of his daring.[55]

Liturgists, unaccustomed to the frank and brutal assessments of the art world, may find this unpleasant, but many congregants have no better opinion of liturgical method acting. Catching the idea at the point of emergence is not *artless* — not if it really is an idea; the spontaneity of a practiced, self-critical mind is not the spontaneity of the casual participant caught off guard in public. Though a fine interpreter can extract profundities even from second-order work, the process of seeking profundity is discriminating and private, and it takes time. When liturgy becomes, as it were, the refrigerator door of the religious community — half-formulated comments given equal weight with written sermons, seminarians' first-draft effusions printed in the prayer books alongside the work of the sages, like toddlers' scribblings posted with lavish praise among museum postcards of the old masters — there is no place for, no definition of, the religious personality beyond the first-grade level.

Liturgists who promote this kind of spontaneity see it as a way to ensure the spiritual equality, the acceptability in God's sight, of everyone present. The principle is sound; it is what James was getting at in his description of the sick soul's helplessness: "What he craves is to be consoled in his very powerlessness, to feel that the spirit of the universe recognizes and secures him, all decaying and failing as he is."[56] But in practice the exercise in spontaneity heavily favors the healthy-minded. It gives the loquacious and unguarded infinite opportunity to be exactly who they are, while the reticent and complicated have an increasing sense that what they have to say is explosive in its intensity, permanently unacceptable. It is no surprise if the reticent sometimes feel there is nowhere to graduate to except orthodoxy, which at least believes in cultivating one's skills. Orthodox repressions and formalized structures of forgiveness face more honestly the prolonged effort toward worthiness that liberal religion merely dismisses. It is unfortunate that orthodoxy essentially confirms the permanence of one's unacceptability, whereas liberal religion's acceptance is not as unconditional as it claims, but is given on condition that one break the "silent loyalty oath" to take one's experience seriously. The two religious styles divide up between them what should be a perpetual interplay of tolerance and rigor.

Liturgy and Violence

Liturgy is like art, and unlike psychotherapy, in that *it rehearses simultaneously the trauma and its cure*. It can be infinitely repeated because it both recreates and makes a way through the suffering. Its structure is cyclical rather than linear, moving from distress to stability not over a period of years but within the same daily and weekly and yearly round of services. It may have a highly dramatic structure like the Mass or the Passover seder, or a quality of protracted and arduous work as in the Jewish morning service or the monastic singing of the hours. (The Hebrew words *avodah*, divine service, and *avdut*, slavery, share a common root.) In either case its structure is ultimately not explanatory but narrative. It is, perhaps, a pre-Enlightenment form by nature — which is not to say that reason is alien to it: only that it proceeds by enactment, not recommendation.

Steiner's *Real Presences*, which asserts the indelibly religious nature of secular art, identifies a particular quality of wounding or woundedness as the religious dimension of works to which we feel compelled to return. "There was, presumably, no need of books or of art in Eden. That which has been indispensable thereafter has communicated the urgency of a great hurt."[57] Even in the absence of prayer or practice, art serves as a quasi-liturgical memorial to lonely suffering. Unless prayer and practice themselves somehow serve as such a memorial, they will not seem indispensable; instead they will puzzle and disappoint. *Avodah* at its most urgent arises as an antidote to the woundedness of *avdut*. "[T]he deliverance," says James, "must come in as strong a form as the complaint, if it is to take effect; and that seems a reason why the coarser religions, revivalistic, orgiastic, with blood and miracles and supernatural operations, may possibly never be displaced. Some constitutions need them too much."[58] Formal liturgy is subtler than that, but psychologically no less drastic.

Just as a sense of the numinous cannot be taught in the standard Sunday-school curriculum, the pathos of shakenness cannot be taught by ordinary pedagogical methods. It must be induced. The story of the *Akedah*, the binding of Isaac in Genesis 22, may serve in Jewish liturgy as such an induction. The story appears in the annual cycle of Torah readings and on the second day of Rosh Hashanah, and also in the Orthodox daily morning liturgy: men bind the leather straps of the *tefillin* on their arms and heads and shortly afterward read the *Akedah*. This daily recollection of an act of inexplicable divine violence — which some modern commentators flatfootedly but not therefore inaccurately call an act of child abuse — seems equally inexplicable as ritual: why this, of all things, and why first thing in the morning? But as some survivors of severe childhood trauma have found, there may be no palliation for suffering so convincing as its reenactment under controlled conditions. Reenactment may include not only therapeutic abreaction but wildcat lay therapies like self-inflicted injury and sadomasochism; the daily reading of a biblical passage, however uncanny and terrible a passage, is relatively civilized by comparison. Those who take the lesson of *Akedah* to be the proscription of human sacrifice are half right, but only half right: the lesson — so far as there is a cleanly identifiable lesson — is not simply that child sacrifice is proscribed, nor even that a child badly used need not grow up to perpetuate the abuse. It is *also* that the event, having happened, locks itself in the memory half-comprehended and must be recalled: again and again, on our terms, in the hope of its being assimilated. We read the story not because we approve or accept its violence, but because we have to integrate it and cannot. The self-binding of *tefillin* is not explicitly connected in the liturgy to Isaac's binding, and for anyone not in need of the connection may never be; nonetheless it is a voluntary, communal and repeated enactment of Isaac's near-sacrifice. Soon after waking, perhaps after difficult dreams, the wordless physical sense of being softly held by the *tefillin* and by the covenant gradually works its consolation, with no direct mention of consolation; the repetition of the story both acknowledges the depth of the damage and demonstrates the possibility of survival. Used over time, the ritual is a subtle transformation of trauma into work.

In Christian liturgy, the Crucifixion holds a more central place: the redemptive sacrifice that reverses the downward trend of human corruption, the fulcrum on which history turns. The image is absolutely ambiguous in its effects, being as liable historically to incite crusade or pogrom as to induce private grief and repentance. The risk is built into the Gospels and Christian liturgy that Christians whose perception cannot be prolonged by the image of Jesus' suffering to the point of seeing their own faults will become murderously enraged at the supposed faults of others — other Christians as well as Jews and Muslims: a periodic degeneration into the kitsch of revenge that is the worst irony of a religion which enjoins nonviolence and infinite forgiveness. In spite of this, the effects of the Holy Week liturgy are far different than this for introspective and self-critical people. The "shakenness" of believing oneself in any degree responsible for the death of the incarnate God, and the absolute *Verfremdung* of the empty tomb and the risen Christ, induce humility and wonder. The violent act that Christianity imagines at the crux of the moral universe and the center of time (the very numbering of the years reversing itself at the savior's birth) is overdetermined to a degree that cannot be simplified; its logic is not in the theology but in the catharsis. Recent efforts to rewrite Atonement theology so as to make the Crucifixion merely a human political atrocity and not a reconciling act of divine violence are well meant, but cannot touch the imagination; emotionally it would make better sense to extend the old paradox *felix culpa* not just to Adam's sin but to the roles of Judas, Caiaphas, Pilate, "the Jews," and God himself in bringing about the sacrifice, with praise replacing millennia of blame. Theology is rhetorical, but God is dialectical; "I make peace and create evil" is not reducible to a rational theology.

But the trauma of evil is not the worst we have to encounter. "The worst is not, so long as we can say, 'This is the worst.'" The trauma of good is in its way even more dreadful. We could define God out of existence — locate God inwardly as an apperception of the universe within the self, fold the transcendent entirely into the immanent — and we would still feel the pressure of difference, the human other's uncanny distance from the self. Levinas speaks of the face of the other as obligating, the trauma of the other's presence as a wound: "The one is exposed to the other as a skin is exposed to what wounds it, as a cheek is offered to the smiter....This being torn up from oneself in the core of one's unity...[t]his pain, this underside of skin, is a nudity more naked than all destitution."[59] There are times when we tolerate the other as one tolerates extreme heat or cold, in pain and at absolute risk. The shock sustained in encountering the otherness of the other, the breaking in upon one's consciousness of another's exigent need, is as disruptive to the personality and as permanent in its effects as the experience of violence. To recognize another's suffering — perhaps even to inflict that suffering and then recognize it — is to be destroyed in one's essential ease with oneself.

Not everyone suffers war trauma or domestic violence; everyone is assailed by the otherness of the other. If trauma in its common definition consists partly in having one's needs radically unmet, violated by another's cruelty or neglect, for Levinas the trauma of the other is the violation of one's own secure boundaries by another's *legitimate* needs: the need of the hungry for food, the naked for clothing, the homeless for shelter, the friendless for love. The trauma of ethics is seldom spoken of; perhaps it lies too deep in all of us, in some fragment of childhood cognition too early for words, when we first saw that we could do harm. But each of us, in our moral sense, carries the hairtrigger reactiveness that is the mark of past trauma, an insistence prior to words or moral precepts that *there are some things you just don't do*. Abraham Heschel speaks of the prophets' extremity of outrage, their shrillness, "one octave too high," at the obscenity of the most ordinary civic injustices.[60] Levinas speaks of the "pre-original hold" of the good over us, its choosing us before we choose it.[61] Steiner says, terribly, that the grudge of Christian Europe against the Jews was not that they killed God but that they invented him; Hitler's remark that "conscience is a Jewish invention" shows the depth of the resentment,[62] though it presupposes inaccurately that conscience can be eradicated. But the West is too deeply habituated to "the blackmail of perfection," in Steiner's phrase:[63] we both resist and are drawn to the visionary goal that we cannot meet with our utmost effort, yet cannot cease to desire.

In this light — or this darkness — it is worth reconsidering the violence of religious language, and whether it may after all be necessary. Not so much the triumphant violence of God as the warrior king or the lachrymose violence of Jesus as the suffering servant, and not the violence of those who think themselves righteous toward the unrighteous, but Hosea's conjugal torment, the searing of Isaiah's lips with the live coal, Francis Thompson's "hound of heaven," T. S. Eliot's "Christ the tiger." God's unpredictable capacity for both good and evil is, if nothing else, an incisive metaphor for the full range of our experience. The trauma of goodness — one might even call it the evil of goodness — produces its own symptoms, of which violent metaphor is one. John Donne — it will be remembered that Donne is one of Stanley Fish's exemplars of dialectical writing, and that Fish speaks of the experience of reading dialectical writing as humiliating — knew his way around violent metaphor; his sonnet "Batter my heart," recently the subject of much uncomprehending theological commentary, shows the extent of it:

> Batter my heart, three-person'd God; for you
> As yet but knock, breathe, shine, and seek to mend;
> That I may rise, and stand, o'erthrow me, and bend
> Your force, to break, blow, burn and make me new.

I, like an usurp'd town, to another due,
Labour to admit you, but Oh, to no end,
Reason your viceroy in me, me should defend,
But is captiv'd, and proves weak or untrue,
Yet dearly I love you, and would be lovèd fain,
But am betroth'd unto your enemy,
Divorce me, untie, or break that knot again,
Take me to you, imprison me, for I
Except you enthrall me, never shall be free,
Nor ever chaste, except you ravish me.[64]

"A great hurt." The poem has been held up by feminists and students of nonviolence as an unseemly and pernicious image of God, which condones self-abasement and intimate violence in the name of religion. They mistake for the pathos of glory what is clearly the pathos of shakenness. The dynamic of commanding God to break you is something more complex than a dumb docility in the face of a brutal religion. The violent and commanding voice in the sonnet is not God's but Donne's: the poet is in charge, and ferociously impatient with God. It would be impossible to deny the escalating violence of *imprison, enthrall, ravish* in the last three lines, yet this is not the hardening of the heart but a terrible plea for its softening: not violence conceived as punishment but violence sought as a desperate measure of relief. The eroticism of the final sestet is the intimate speech of one who trusts his hearer. To demand to be wounded by a good God is not to sanction violence by bad humans; the point of "ravish" at that climactic place is its ambiguity in our common speech between helplessness and consent, and its absolute clarity in the poem not merely as consent but as fierce invitation. In real extremity of either kind, the cry of pleasure cannot be distinguished from the cry of pain; formal liturgy, too reticent to make its speakers cry aloud for either reason, must still make a way for them to cry within, or else give up its holdings in the tenderest and most wounded centers of the brain.

Can the language of sanity ever equal the language of desperation? Is the origin of liturgy always in craziness and extremity, never in security and stability? Maybe so. Consciousness itself may arise only at the point of disturbance; sanity may always be something achieved, not given. Slavoj Žižek, following the lead of certain cognitive scientists, is "convinced that consciousness originates with something going terribly wrong — even at a most personal level. For example, when do we become aware of something, fully aware? Precisely at the point where something no longer functions properly or not in the expected way."[65] In that sense consciousness has a built-in, intrinsic quality of "hurt"; we are hard-wired for what C. S. Lewis once called "the inconsolable wound with which man is born."[66] The story of the "great hurt" of Eden, the eating of the forbidden fruit and the expulsion from paradise, proposes consciousness as indeed *daat tov v'ra* (knowledge of good and evil), good lost and evil got. To be conscious is to be conscious of what is lost; any stability worth the name must start from that knowledge.

By disallowing discomfort, it is thus *consciousness itself* that kitsch retards. The element of uncertainty, of emergence — sometimes of emergency — that characterizes children's private speech, adult therapeutic speech, and "dialectical" prose, is the mark of consciousness disturbed and in search of language. Recalling Ratey's assertion that the neurological work of making associative connections increases intelligence, the stasis of kitsch when substituted for associative work actively stunts intelligence. Žižek remarks that "from a strict evolutionary standpoint, consciousness is a kind of mistake — a malfunction of evolution — and...out of this mistake a miracle emerged. That is to say, consciousness developed as an unintended by-product that acquired a kind of second-degree survivalist function. Basically, consciousness is not something which enables us to function better."[67] Whether evolution can be said to have malfunctioned in a peculiarly successful species — or to have done something it had not "intended" — consciousness must be cultivated as a miracle that remedies disruption and loss. The only thing that can compensate for the pain of consciousness is more consciousness. In Scarry's terms, the forms of "controlled discomfort" (building, making, art, science, speech) that mitigate the "aversiveness" of pain represent the imaginative response of consciousness to the hurt that made it arise.[68] In therapeutic terms, language restructures consciousness from a disordered and unpredictable state to a state in which one can love and work. "Of Consciousness, her awful Mate / The Soul cannot be rid," Dickinson said; if we repeat the trauma of consciousness in our rituals it is from the sense of its mastering importance.

Jacob Neusner speaks of "the enchantments of Judaism": the ritual words and acts that mediate between *is* and *as if* to transform the daily into the sacred, and random vaguely Jewish individuals into God's people. *Avodah* in its widest sense becomes an act of imagination, an entry into "life lived as metaphor."[69] Neusner calls theology a cognitive science, an assessment more trusting than I am willing to make, but liturgy is certainly a cognitive art: it moves us by slow degrees from repetition as curse and affliction to repetition as blessing. Through liturgical practice the trauma of ethics becomes not "the blackmail of perfection" which sets an unreachable standard, but the law that is very near to us, in our mouths and in our hearts. The knowledge of good and evil — of extremity, and the chance of surviving extremity — may be all that makes our own goodness seem desirable. Nothing else makes so clear to us the reason for moral effort: the perishable face and voice of the other, which disclose to us all that we can know of the imperishable.

The word "enchantment" is almost beyond reclamation; its almost inevitable association with kitsch for children makes it immediately suspect. Neusner uses the word accurately, but at some risk. Donald Kalsched, a Jungian analyst specializing in trauma therapy, raises the ante by using the same word in the context of mental illness. He distinguishes the "bewitchment" of misery or madness from the "enchantment" of a life in which moral choice and the exercise of one's powers become consciously possible. Enchantment is "what fairy tales mean when they end 'happily ever after'"[70] — no unreal state of euphoria, to be punctured after the wedding when the prince still shows symptoms of froggishness, but the joy of being set at last in one's place, beyond the adversities of bewitchment, freed for the normal business of living and dying. The violence of fairy tales, as Bettelheim and others have pointed out, is far from gratuitous; it is an imaginative negotiation of conditions that nothing but imagination can solve. Enchantment is not a fairy-dust rescue from the unacceptable, from "shit and death"; it is the triumph of intelligence, courtesy and courage over the cruel and the loathsome. The violence of the Hebrew Bible operates at a more complex cultural level than the fairy tale, and makes a much steeper approach to the happy ending, but its progression from the covenant cut in the flesh to the covenant written on the heart is as surely conceived as the fairy tale's progress from bewitchment to enchantment: as intimate a wound, as restorative a purpose.

Deep calleth unto deep: the deep of our misery unto the deep of thy mercy.[71] (St. Bernard's gloss on Psalm 42:9, which Lancelot Andrewes of the King James Bible committee wrote into his private prayer book: what the "elite" say to themselves when no one is listening is worth investigating.) Without the acknowledgment of misery there is no foothold for mercy. Religion, art and psychology intersect in this articulation of pain, which is not an exceptional or specialized use of liturgy but one of its steadiest purposes. We came crying hither. Our purpose even as infants — the whole thrust of our development and education — is to change the cry into language. If liturgy insists on reminding us of the origins of our consciousness in pain, it is not so that pain may govern but so that *articulation* may govern; not to make us predators but to show us how to endure having been the prey. Some readers are bound to see my argument as a refusal of mercy, the setting of a deliberate barrier between the wounded soul and its consolation. Not at all. The barrier is already there. The work of liturgy, like the work of therapy, is to find a way through and around it: a way from the world as it is to a world that can contain us. The fundamental aim of ritual is the replication of humaneness; the more effort, the more consolation.

Chapter 5

Putting the Id Back in Liturgy

If religious enthusiasm be considered not so much an opiate as
an amphetamine...

—Nigel Spivey, *Enduring Creation*

For there is not a word in my tongue, but thou, O Lord, know-
est it altogether.

—Ps. 139:3 (Coverdale)

The "talking cure" has been accused of talking too much: of bringing privacies too much into the open, of making indirection and
subtlety culturally obsolete, of short-circuiting introspection. Steiner classes psychoanalysis with the mass media and the telephone as
a destroyer of "concentrated linguistic internality,"[1] as if with the
simultaneous ascendancy of frankness and mass communication
adult inner speech (which is to say, *thought*) has necessarily become
thinner and less substantial. But there is a difference between psychological theory as a topic of dinner conversation, or therapy as a
shortcut to better "adjustment," and the reconstruction of personality in cases of desperate mental dismay. In talk that really does cure,
the disclosures are neither facile nor public.

And in the frankest social surroundings there are still unsayable
things: privacies that must be protected, intimacies for which words
cannot be found, strong feelings inadmissible in one's own circle,
fears no one else can comprehend. We talk out the troubles of our

relationships and find them still unsolved; we fall in love with people we cannot have, and must maintain silence; we learn other people's secrets and cannot disclose them. We fear an impending disaster — social or military or planetary — that may or may not come to pass, and must try to remain sane and intelligible in the face of anxiety. We adopt a political or religious allegiance, renounce the requisite forms of recreation or food or love or prayer, and conceive for them an inconsolable and inadmissible nostalgia. Even reputation is not a thing of the past — not even in tell-all contemporary America; its forms shift, but we remain painfully conscious of what people think of us. We need circumlocution.

Moral imagination itself compels silence in most of these cases. To keep faith with the demands of our circumstances we must sometimes refuse opportunities for speech. But moral imagination also provides a way out, in the images that arise when direct speech is impossible. Analogy and metaphor become our allies; a cigar is no longer just a cigar nor a spade a spade. The unsatisfied need for speech is channeled into the conduits of thought, where it travels with greater force and leaks out at any seam or pinhole. The more urgent the problem, the more fiercely the mind works against its insolubility; it is driven to discover figures of thought and speech, and then driven by them.

The most compelling liturgy does not yield all its meaning at once. It needs to withhold something, so as to reveal itself over years of use. Some of it needs to be impenetrable and never reveal itself. It must present something for everyone to understand, but nothing is wasted if not everything is understood by every person at every time. It has hiding places. Just as "covert processes" play a part in the therapeutic relationship, where a metaphor imposed by the therapist can provoke the patient's silent resistance, in liturgy too "verbal communication underrepresents subjective meaning."[2] Language imposed without the worshiper's consent can set off a mutinous search for alternative meanings. This is as much a phenomenon of the new liturgies as of the old; some of the most apparently open and guileless liturgical writing is some of the most covertly authoritarian in its preemptive resolution of ambiguities, while some of the most openly coercive leaves room for speculation. If the sense of a word as distinct from its plain meaning is, as Vygotsky said, "the sum of all the psychological events aroused in our consciousness by the word," liturgy becomes a collaborative metaphor in ways that its writers will never suspect. Where liturgists are most careful to give a word one permissible meaning, other meanings will begin to cling to the word without their consent.

The extreme delicacy with which private meanings attach themselves to public liturgical statements makes them impossible to defend, especially to secure, confident clergy on a mission: how can one oppose egalitarianism or rationality, reinforced by mild-mannered collegial consensus, any more than one can oppose militant orthodoxy enforced by the Star Chamber? Nonetheless the subjective experience of liturgy is its true life. Only sometimes do programmatic changes like the use of female pronouns ring true with our private meanings, and only when the new usage matches a need in the personality; just as easily they can interfere, scrambling the signals or triggering a resistance that may surprise even ourselves. The patient who said, "The unconscious is more real; it's more enduring; and it has endured me" was not looking for "inclusive language" in the usual sense.

Words, in liturgy, must substitute for almost the whole realm of touch. They must accomplish on the bodies of strangers everything that strangers are forbidden to accomplish: the consolation of a mother's arms and breasts, the strength of a father's back, the shock of an enemy's blow, the igniting honor of a lover's touch. After our earliest years there is very little place for the physical in our emotional lives with strangers, the handshake and the polite hug being about the extent of it. Adults (with a few exceptions made for close friends and kin) must be prepared to accept either full sexuality or false heartiness: too much truth or not enough. The austere and restrained physical acts permitted in liturgy, like the reception of the Eucharist or the kissing of the Torah, become powerful because they *are* eating and kissing in a context that otherwise forbids physical intimacy. The words that surround such liturgical acts need a power consistent with that reserve.

There is a tendency, even at the communal level, for the meanings of words to alter, and to accrue — as the Kaddish began as a prayer for the conclusion of study and became a prayer for the conclusion of life, and "How goodly are your tents, O Jacob" began as a pagan prophet's curse-turned-blessing[3] and became the opening prayer of the morning synagogue service. Liturgical phrases acquire ironic uses: *mea culpa* for minor instances of neglect, "Blessed are you, Lord our God, king of the universe, who gives strength to the weary" as an impromptu blessing over caffeine, *The Happy Issue* as the title of an Episcopal church newsletter. As simple a phrase as "renew our days as of old"[4] picks up new specificity in a time of persecution or war; in a time of private loss or uncertainty — a financial reversal, a protracted illness, an impasse with a lover or a child — it picks up extraneous and keenly felt personal meaning. But the origins of the private meaning lie deeper.

Consider how anguish is sometimes relieved by the silence of indifferent nature: the great calm that does not notice one's pain, and which provides a kind of primitive healing by simply not being hostility. The experience is common, but has no theological standing; its liturgical expression is muted. "There is no speech nor language" — the silence of the heavens in Psalm 19 is not so much a cause for wonder on its own terms as a preface to the consciousness-restructuring properties of the law and justice of God. Job's near-silence after God speaks to him from the whirlwind is a kind of convalescence from words. As the voice from the whirlwind implies, the silence of nature is morally ambiguous; our rectitude means nothing to it, our failures reap no condemnation. The world permits us to go on living and asks no questions. The indecent, cheerful barbarity of our flourishing bodies, battening on the refuse of nature and history; the delicate Polish forests, rising out of the ash of the Jewish dead; there is no speech nor language that will contain both the gratefulness and the corruption of simply being alive. As the Kaddish in Judaism enacts in ritual what we do after a death — go on praising, whether we want to or not — perhaps the really central mystery of the Christian Mass is that we go on eating and drinking after having sinned. Jesus is dispensable in the equation; the real action of the Mass is the link between confession and communion, the crushing recognition of one's own shame and the acceptance of food. Historically the Catholic Church has made confession a method of intimate institutional control as the necessary passport to communion, but the legends of saints who subsisted on nothing but the sacramental wafer suggest another pattern. In an acute condition of shame we cannot eat; in a chronic condition of shame we may starve ourselves, until we throw ourselves on the mercy of the universe — whereupon the universe responds by *continuing normal life*, ignoring our shame and supplying our daily needs. It may be only the indifference of a creation too large to be concerned with our daily needs, but we take it as grace: the universe's astonishing propensity to forgive and restore, not weighing our merits but pardoning our offenses. The Mass encodes the terrible persistence of our will to live, in its full juxtaposition of humble dignity and moral collapse: we are sinners and opportunists, and at the same time vulnerable human beings who get hungry. "After Auschwitz one can no longer eat lunch, either; but one does."[5]

Liturgy cannot approach such matters directly: not only because such a reading violates the stated intent of the Mass, but because a direct approach is too clumsy. One need only imagine a responsive reading full of expressions like *eating disorders* and *low self-esteem* to see how abjectly it would fail. Ritual must replicate experience through its structure. The alternation of Sabbath and workdays

— particularly in its original, almost utilitarian Jewish form — creates a sound structure for living with ambiguity: the simple physical rhythm of work and rest accommodates the permanent intellectual and spiritual conflict between outrage at the world's imperfection and awe at its loveliness. For six days the world is a wreck of political corruption, economic struggle, social and moral vacuity, failure and loss; on the seventh day it is perfect. For six days we struggle to endure and repair the disaster around us, on the seventh we eat and sing and make love. The ritual is so obviously a construct that it ought to be incredible; the very language reflects its artifice — we "*make* Shabbes." Yet making Shabbes every week establishes an atmosphere as dependable as sunrise and sunset, or the phases of the moon. Moral effort and transfixed gratitude have their own rhythm — indeed, must be kept from destroying each other — and the very artifice of the Sabbath confirms the possibility of setting reliable bounds between fiercely opposing emotional needs. But it need never be said analytically in the ritual.

The quirkiness of the subjective reading may threaten established assumptions from all sides. The gendered morning blessings in orthodox Judaism — the man's "who has not made me a woman" and the woman's "who has made me according to your will" — have consistently been read by their critics as expressions of male repugnance and female resignation; any attempt to soften them or explain them otherwise has seemed the most obtuse and reactionary whitewashing. Yet in profound privacy the blessings take on mischievous life. A woman on the threshold of ecstasy (it does not much matter whether she is with a man, with another woman, or alone) may find no other words for her gratitude at her own physical construction. (*Ratzon*, the word translated "will," is sometimes used with overtones of desire, so that the blessing can be read "who made me as you wanted me," or even "who made me for your pleasure.") A heterosexual man in love, feeling showered with the graces of an otherness he cannot provide for himself, may pray his words gratefully too — with the sense "I love women so much I'm glad not to be one." The paired blessings conceal a secret: it may be a secret even from some heterosexual couples, who walk through the normative stages of marriage and prayer without gratitude, but a secret is not invalidated by not being perceived. It remains and awaits discovery. Resignation is certainly a possible reading of the woman's blessing, and repugnance or a homoerotic fastidiousness of the man's, *but the blessings do not interpret themselves*; they are terse, expressionless, using the refuge of the liturgical monotone to mask the strongest emotions from those who have no right to know them. They allow several readings without comment — without "privileging" any one over the others. (This is consonant with rabbinic tradition, where the word *b'rit*, covenant, may be used for everything from the sworn relationship between God and Israel with its heavy obligations, to the rite of circumcision that is the sign of that relationship, to the site of circumcision wherewith we are begotten.) In liturgy, intimate secrets can be simultaneously spoken and concealed.

It may be objected that such readings are outrageously beside the point, or are merely indecent; yet as a rule no one has to know about them but the person who thinks of them, and only the invasion of privacy by inexpert and insistent revision makes them necessary to speak of at all. Does the privacy of such readings render them illegitimate? Are they so inadmissible as possibilities as to be impermissible as actualities? Must the privacy of one's own id be sacrificed for the common good? So far as liturgy is (true to its etymology) the people's work, this is where it knows what the people are: not a flock of sheep to be herded by community standards, not "the masses" to be denied the bourgeois luxury of an inner life, but a collection of unruly minds thinking away on their own, making happy puns after a night of love or bitter comments on history. It is not necessary for all the puns to be brought into the open or all the interpretations aired; private readings are not esoteric readings, to be imparted to a group of initiates. They arrive on their own and belong to their owners; there is no "the" meaning. There is only a series of meanings subsidiary to the intended one, arising from analogical play and as casual or as forceful as we make them at any given time. A democratic view of liturgy requires as a principle that everyone be allowed their interpretations; an orthodox view allows privacy. Either view must concede that our thoughts are our own.

Recent attempts at inclusiveness — the naming of the previously disenfranchised and of hitherto unnamed distresses — have been so earnestly literal as to leave the analogical impulse with little to do. Episcopal priest Vienna Cobb Anderson's occasional prayers for the emergencies of pastoral work are among the most generous and copious of these efforts. Anderson makes no claims for her gifts as a writer; her aim was to supplement the omissions of "the period of sweeping liturgical change during the 1960s and 1970s, [when] words were shuffled on paper by scholars, but the cries of seekers for a new language of prayer went largely unheard,"[6] a claim with which one may sympathize. Her prose is moved by the needs of the sufferer and not of the institution, which gives it emotional directness; one can imagine the prayers, used in their original context and animated by Anderson's considerable energy, as having had power. But there is virtually no sense of a lineage of experience, of the biblical culture that originally shaped Jewish and Christian concern for the needs of the sufferer, or of the poetic culture that allows one experience to see itself by analogy with another. Anderson's 1991 book of prayers addresses many intimate disasters: Prayer for a Divided Family, Prayer for a Child Who Has Been Molested, Prayer for Children Killing Children, Prayer for Those Who Hate Their Parents — the abused, the neglected, the missing, the victims of terrorists, the terrorists, the sick in a long procession of anguish (birth defects, cancer, dementia, stroke, hysterectomy, mastectomy, amputation, AIDS). Taken cumulatively, even the table of contents gives not a welcome sense of the naming of the previously unnamed but a numbing sense of the futility of all prayer. There will always one more condition that was not addressed, one more overlooked illness, one more love that dare not speak its name; one has the sense of queuing up for one's morsel of God's attention, rather than coming into the presence of an all-comprehending regard. Inclusion is understood as mere accumulation. Allusiveness is virtually absent; the prayers offer the sufferer no companions in suffering — no Cain and Abel, no Abraham and Isaac, no Rachel and Leah, no David and Bathsheba, no Amnon and Tamar, no Hosea and Gomer; no Jeremiah compelled in childhood to prophesy and crying to God "you have raped me and I am overcome;"[7] no woman with the issue of blood, no man with the demon whose name is Legion, no "out of the depths I cry unto thee," no "let the day perish wherein I was born." Anderson felt the existing language of worship — the old and the new — merely as burdensome, claiming that it "neither names our dreams, struggles, or sorrows, nor offers us the consolation of feeling named or affirmed as full members of the Body of Christ."[8] The implication is that subjectivity can have no companions, that contemporary experience admits of no prototypes, that to give one's subjectivity a cultural prototype is not to expand it to infinity but to diminish it to nothing.

Yet the use of old language for one's own purposes is vastly liberating, and allows the full range of emotion from open defiance to a delicate *chutzpah*. A 1786 prayer book compiled by Giuseppe Coen for his wife Yehudit, and recently edited by Nina Beth Cardin, enlists the psalms to orchestrate the end of the period of menstrual abstinence observed by orthodox Jews with a dignified ingenuity so striking as to be clearly an instance of private meaning rather than patriarchal control.[9] There are lines for protection as the woman walks through the streets to the ritual bath (in the dark, for modesty's sake, and thus at some risk): "Guard me like the apple of your eye, hide me in the shadow of your wings;"[10] "I lift my eyes to the hills; from whence comes my help?…By day the sun will not strike you, nor the moon by night;"[11] "You need not fear the terror by night, or the arrow that flies by day."[12] The final psalm in the series is the twenty-third: as the woman kisses the mezuzah at her own door and prepares to reenter the house where her husband waits, "thy rod and thy staff they comfort me" and "my cup runneth over" become charged with erotic meaning.[13] Tikva Frymer-Kensky, in her recent *Motherprayer*, uses the same method for the experience of pregnancy, strikingly assigning images of the exodus from Egypt (*Mitzrayim*, the narrow place) and the crossing of the Red Sea to the child at the time of birth, along with lines from the psalms: "I will walk before the Lord in the lands of the living;"[14] "Open the gates of righteousness; I will pass through them and praise the Lord."[15] Historically, biblical cultures link unselfconsciously the humblest joys of the body with the regard and protection of God; they also handle texts with a great deal of sophistication. There is no reason this tradition cannot be continued by a modern and skeptical sensibility, and employed for the distresses of illness and trauma and history as well as the happy occasions of love and birth. The psalms belong intimately to anyone who can read them; they are public property meant also for private use.

We owe an allegiance to our development; it gives us an independent island of judgment in the midst of the collective. Even the id is not merely the source of sin and unruliness, any more than the superego is merely the force of repression; both are parts of the self that, like feeling and thought, must learn to cooperate. Jewish thought presupposes that nothing good can be accomplished without, as it were, a leavening of the evil impulse: the Mishnah declares that "one must bless for the evil as one blesses for the good, as it is written: 'And you shall love the Lord your God with all your heart and with all your soul and with all your might.' 'With all your heart' — with both impulses, the good impulse and the evil impulse."[16] The Midrash adds that without the evil impulse — in this instance essentially identified with sexual desire — "a man would not build a house, take a wife, beget children, or engage in commerce."[17] Philip Roth's Portnoy, who wanted to "put the id back in Yid," was no talmudist; the id had never been missing. In Jewish folk usage, a *mitzvah* is a commandment not in the austere sense but in a joyful one: the unconstrained libido enlisted by the voice from Sinai in the task of making more justice.

To the alert energies of the evil impulse, historical liturgies are always yielding unforeseen relevance; some indelible image or turn of phrase may refuse to go away, some politically dubious prayer may be discovered to have meant something all along besides triumphalism or misogyny. It is difficult to say what might *not* be relevant. When ingenuity and imagination are ruled out of common liturgical use, or reserved for graduate study, a prayer book becomes merely another instance of benign censorship — dreary, directive, untrustworthy from the start. Naturally it is risky to confront other imaginations; other people's religious ardors, like other people's sexual attachments, may astonish and disturb. But so may one's own over the course of a lifetime, and learning to live with disturbance is part of adult life. To cut the id out of liturgy may even be to undercut the conscience to a certain degree. The id that has license to satirize or puncture, and on occasion to circumvent, the superego will keep it from making impossible demands; eventually it may offer it unexpected corroboration, and prove the strongest ally in achieving the impossible. The partnership between id and superego is where everything happens, in liturgy as in life: the superego is allowed its full moral force without compromising the physical force of the id, a bond between desire and restraint that is difficult to surpass for durability.

Private revelation has never been popular with religious authorities, and liberal authorities are not very different in this regard; theological surveillance seems to come with the territory. Of course authorities like their authority, but they also have a legitimate fear: that the subjective response will divert the individual from legitimate obedience, that the playful backwaters of the mind will prove more fascinating than the intent of the text and the current of communal obligation. But there is more than one way to arrive at a sense of commandedness. For some people the sheer collectivity of a moral system is enough to compel acceptance: this is what the community does, and a sense of order and courtesy requires one to do the same. For others the moral imperatives they discover for themselves, in secret and far from help, are the first and great commandments; only the discovery of these same imperatives embedded in the structure of ritual gives the ritual any authority. The "silent loyalty oath taken during the loneliest of times, an oath never to forget" is not exclusive to sufferers from trauma; or rather the trauma of goodness, suffered alone, compels us to the same oath. We do not willingly cede our difficult experience to the simplifying clarities of a system.

A mature subjectivity has links to collective reality; it retains its independence, but binds itself by the ties of allusion and analogy to other subjectivities and to the tradition. Some forms of subjectivity do fall short of mature consciousness: the "simple faith" that solves problems by sticking a pin in the Bible and reasoning from a random text, or at the other extreme the militantly narrow imagination that cannot find "relevance" in anything that does not address it by name. But between these extremes — or beyond them, in a third cognitive dimension — is a subjectivity that is both rational and open to surprise. We learn our morals much as we learn our vocabulary: not so much through disembodied lists and definitions as through an experienced context, made up of both life experience and the vicarious experience of art and narrative. Subjectivity is not a kind of stubbornness or resistance but a kind of proprioception, by which we locate ourselves in the moral world.

A recent hymn by Thomas Troeger grasps, to some extent, and addresses liturgically the symbiosis between subjectivity and command. The hymn is based on two New Testament texts on freedom — John 8:32, "And ye shall know the truth, and the truth shall make you free," and I Peter 2:16, "As free, and not using your liberty for a cloke of maliciousness, but as the servants of God":

Eagles' spiralings comply
To the densities of sky
And the ceaseless downward tug
Of the earth's deep iron core
And what ligaments can bear
Tensing flesh and hollow bone
Stiff against the rush of air.

Lord, you made earth's iron core
And the hollow bone and wind,
And you taught the birds to soar,
Showing how their wings must bend
For the mass and speed and force
Of the air to lift their weight
As they glide and carve their course.

In our muscle and our bone
What the eagle knows is known.
Help the heart now, Lord, to learn
That the freedom it desires,
Like all soaring flight, requires
That we bend our strength and skill
To your word and wind and will.

Refrain: Circling, circling,
Swooping, planing,
Rising, rising
Heaven gaining.[18]

The unusual seven-line stanza, the striking off-rhyme of *core* and *bear,* and the rapt contemplation of flight in a world bound by gravity, produce a tensile strength rarely found or attempted in the liturgy of the last forty years. The first stanza can stand beside the best hymns in Christian tradition; it may be as close as a hymn can come to Hopkins's "Windhover." The second stanza begins to lose tension, reiterating in the pedagogical mode what is better said in the dialectical; the third stanza's opening couplet is fully up to the level of the first, but the remainder subsides into nagging homily. In the end Troeger turns out to be making a *distinction*, not an analogy; he has, as it were, presented the linguist's kind of rule at its most compelling, only to flee for safety to the philosopher's. Eagles' spiralings "comply" with the laws of physics, which cannot be broken; our wayward hearts, Troeger implies, want freedom without compliance, and need curbs and goads. He thus brings us down — gently, as before, but with what resignation — from the currents of the sky more or less to the sheepfold. But the shift to edification comes too late: the consciousness has already been restructured by the interplay of freedom and discipline in the first stanza. The cat is already out of the bag, or the eagle out of the cage: not the denial of instinct but *the fulfillment of instinct through practice* perfects the eagle's flight and our moral efforts. Our own cognitive makeup points the way — not inevitably or without the possibility of error, but in its structure: the rapt, calm, responsive intentionality of work done with all one's might. Is it God's will? Is it our will? Does it make sense any longer to ask the question? Troeger clearly understands the principle, but has available only the obedience-school adjurations of earlier Protestant hymnody to sustain it; Blake and Yeats and Dickinson might have served him better. The eagle, says Blake, never lost so much time as when he submitted to learn of the crow.[19]

"What the eagle knows is known," not only in mute bone and sinew but in the articulate mind: not without effort, yet without truculence, the mind responding to the wound of consciousness not by inflicting more wounds but by making more consciousness. A trained subjectivity is continually assessing the relationship between past and present; there is a rigor we seek out, eagerly and with inexhaustible energy. Ian Robinson says of the critic's work: "The critic's search is for the good new life of the language, which he recognizes by its consistency (in its newness) with the best he knows."[20] The

Zohar comments on a line from the Song of Songs: "'Set me as a seal upon your heart.' Why 'as a seal'? When a seal is affixed to a certain place, even after it is taken away a mark is left there, which is permanent; its whole shape and image remain behind."[21]

Subjectivity is too thin to stand by itself — but then it never does stand by itself; it responds to the past and to the erosion of the past, to the needs of other subjectivities singly and in groups, and to the "ceaseless downward tug" of our death, which sets a limit on all vacillation. We are never uninfluenced; our subjectivity is an effort to choose from among the influences, and not to choose wrong. Our past commands us, not only overtly through its moral codes but implicitly through the acts that have hurt and healed us; the present commands us through the decisions it presses on us and through its demand on our own unperfected integrity. The rigors of freedom may not produce tame good behavior: when the as-yet-unmarried Mary consents humbly to the Annunciation, her pregnancy is illegitimate in social terms, with a family resemblance to the widowed Tamar's in Genesis 38 (though Tamar's seduction of her father-in-law requires more initiative and imagination). Compliance with the moral law — the achieve of, the mastery of the thing! — is not always conventional. Freedom of association, in the analogical sense, is a process of recognition, a vigil at the point of emergence: the private meaning breaks the surface of consciousness to become idea and then act.

Blake, in "The Marriage of Heaven and Hell," presents a mock vision, a "memorable fancy," in which he has dinner with Isaiah and Ezekiel and asks them about prophecy:

> Then Ezekiel said: "The philosophy of the east taught the first principles of human perception: some nations held one principle for the origin, and some another: we of Israel taught that the Poetic Genius (as you now call it) was the first principle and all the others merely derivative, which

was the cause of our despising the priests and philosophers of other countries, and prophesying that all gods would at last be proved to originate in ours and to be the tributaries of the Poetic Genius; it was this that our great poet King David desired so fervently and invokes so pathetically, saying by this he conquers enemies and governs kingdoms; and we so loved our God, that we cursed in his name all the deities of surrounding nations, and asserted that they had rebelled; from these opinions the vulgar came to think that all nations would at last be subject to the Jews.

"This," said he, "like all firm persuasions, is come to pass; for all nations believe the Jews' code and worship the Jews' God, and what greater subjection can be?"[22]

The last line, like the snap of a wet towel, is a tweak to the Christian "vulgar" with their habituated resentment of Jewish legalism; for Blake the real import of the Hebrew Bible is a *difficile liberté* more demanding than its moral and ritual code. The prophet and the poet — both handled with tongs by the priest and the theologian — unite in seeing God not essentially as a ruler but as a maker. Poets were once called makers, and just as poetry is language at its most intensified, God is the power of creation at its most intensified. If Mordecai Kaplan proposed a God who is a social construct, Blake offers a God who is an *imaginative* construct: a God for whom propitiation and the usual forms of obedience are less than nothing, who demands the response of our full subjectivity. Blake was no aesthete, at play among the metaphors for their sheer beauty; the moral force of his poems is fierce and knowledgeable. His *Verfremdung* of God to the source of metaphor intends nothing less than to "build Jerusalem in England's green and pleasant land." Nor is his Jerusalem the Kremlin, or even the District of Columbia, but a polity informed by desire and justice at a level that politics has never yet understood. His vision is not theocratic in the mode of either Cromwell or Falwell, imposing religious rule on the unwilling, but is internalized and self-governing. For Blake religious life is no discipline of inhibition and thwarting; our religious obligation is not to abase ourselves before the Poetic Genius but to rise to it. "To Mercy, Pity, Peace and Love" — actions, not attributes, of "the human form divine" — "all pray in their distress."

I have heard evangelicals denounce Blake for "putting man in the place of God," but he is working in a direct line with Reformation subjectivity: the primacy of the individual conscience, the covenant written on the heart. Nor is there anything theologically objectionable to the modern sensibility in his idea of God; in terms of "bare content" Kaplan, or Harold Schulweis with his "predicate theology" which defines God by his trace in the works of creation and in our own humane acts,[23] might have taken it for a model. Scarry's analysis of the God of the Hebrew Bible follows Blake closely at important points; she asserts that the biblical writers, in their prohibition of images and their suspicion of certain kinds of material luxury, were

> engaged in a sustained act of inventing an Artifact so monumental and majestic (however problematic) that it perhaps has no peer in any other single artifact invented by another people: the Old Testament prophecy that this Artifact will eventually compel and absorb the attention of the rest of the world...has not proved inaccurate, and the prohibition against other acts of making can in part be understood as an attempt to prevent the energy of completing this one act of invention from being deflected into more modest outcomes.... [T]his Artifact, God, is itself the pure principle of creating: thus "making" is set apart and honored as the most holy, most privileged, and most morally authoritative of acts.[24]

Scarry's insistence that the imagination is moral to the point of "ethical monotony"[25] is an unexpected stance for someone who has studied the varieties of torture, but it parallels Blake's insistence that "[a] poet, a painter, a musician, an architect: the man or woman who is not one of these is not a Christian." For Blake Christianity is not passive, and imagination is not image-making in a "modest" (and therefore idolatrous) sense. "Without unceasing practice nothing can be done....Practice is art; if you leave off you are lost."[26] This is where the theologians would fail, and why they cannot take Blake's vision for their model: it demands an urgency, an intensity and a moral self-propulsion that their intellectual training has conditioned them against. Blake did not think of God-as-Poetic-Genius as an elegant solution to the problem of unbelief. He thought it could be done, *ha-yom*, today.

In one sense the ineptitude of liturgy — its fundamental and glaring incompetence at dealing with difficult practical conditions, from familial strife to the desperate expediencies of war, from the daily distribution of wealth, food and medicine to the prevention of war and global disaster — is an inbuilt condition of the form. The written-from-the-heart wedding vows full of phrases like "open and honest" and "as long as we both shall love," the nonce-prayers for broken homes and particular ailments by name, the wartime invocations that end in hapless best wishes for our leaders to do God's will, are merely honest admissions, the more honest the more inept, that we have no idea how to handle our responsibilities and that ritual is not the place to find out. We write liturgy rather than run for office, go to medical school, work for the State Department or the soup kitchen, feed the hungry and clothe the naked and house the homeless. Eunuchs for the kingdom of heaven. As long as liturgy thinks of itself as the servant of religion in the professional and limited sense, softening the rough edges of biblical ferocity and pacifying rather than restructuring the consciousness, it will be outranked by all trades and professions and disciplines whose business it is to handle the needs of the day. The masters of the literal will always be better at the literal.

In another sense liturgy has always been an attempt to transform the literal: to bring into our experience something from beyond our experience, to compel consciousness to burst its bounds. If liturgists cannot imagine how to do this in the modern world they must keep trying until they can. "Language in a condition of total significance": religion, when it means anything worth having, is *the world* in a condition of total significance. Poetic language replicates and summons this state, the associative overload of mystical experience, in order to make all things new in our perception and in our actions. When modern liturgy takes seriously the prophetic sensibility — not simply its demand for justice, but the demand for justice made in language that cannot be refused, language from which we cannot hide — then it will have the means, and (so far as possible in an imperfect world) the right, to command us. Then metaphor will have left the realm of moral exhortation and found its right use in moral coherence; the superego will lie down with the id, with none to make them afraid.

And the Lord (the unpronounceable name of God — or say *ha-Shem*, the Name, or whatever else will avoid the sad incompetence of "Poetic Genius" or "Imagination") puts Ezekiel down in the valley of the dead metaphors, and behold, they are very dry. Prophesy to the bones, he says, *ben adam* (son of Adam, son of man, human, mortal, a title heavy with senses). And Ezekiel prophesies, and the bones reassemble, "bone to his bone." Analogy to analogy, tenor to vehicle, memory to imagination, they connect; the flesh comes up on the bones, and the skin covers them, but they do not yet breathe.

But it appears she lives, though yet she speak not. Shakespeare's resurrection scene, in the last act of the *Winter's Tale*: Hermione, falsely accused of adultery by her husband Leontes sixteen years ago and believed to have been dead all that time, is presented to him as a statue and brought to life. The vision of the dry bones, but in private life: a resurrection equally beyond hope, the overbearing Paulina stage-managing the event, the spectators awestruck, the tension drawn to the breaking-point as Leontes' longing is stirred to its full anguish. It is rare to see the scene convincingly played; there is a certain self-consciousness about enacting a miracle on the modern stage. How can the wronged Hermione bring herself to accept the broken Leontes? How will the women in the audience stand for it? And again, how can the wronged God bring himself to accept the broken Israel, however repentant? And how will the wronged Israel stand for that, and should Israel not demand a broken and repentant God? But the nature of a miracle is its impossibility: the shift by which the natural order turns over, working deliverance in the midst of the earth.

Prophesy to the *ruah*, says the Lord (spirit *and* wind *and* breath, as in many languages, since mortals lose our souls with our breath); and Ezekiel prophesies, and the bones live and stand up. *I will open your graves, O my people*, declares the Lord. *O, she's warm!* cries Leontes. We do not believe, not us, not literally, not after the twentieth century, that God will open the graves of the Jews; the desperate policies of the state of Israel and the high birth rate of the very orthodox both attest to it. Nor do we believe we will get our dead lovers back. The laws of physics prevent it; our bodies are prepared to accept it. But we would like to see the metaphor that would try it.

God — who may be all that is left of that metaphor — himself seems a shattered idol. The death-of-God theologians — poor literalists who thought all those descriptions of God's goodness and mercy were accurate portraits and not anxious reminders, and so were capable of disillusion — stand about helplessly with the liturgists, trying to match one piece with another. All the king's horses and all the king's men. Little do they know his powers of recovery, or trust their own resources. Shakespeare's other resurrection scene, in the fourth act of *Lear*, has the disinherited Edgar — who has spent most of the play disguised as a Tom-o'-Bedlam, wandering with the outcast Lear's entourage — encounter his father blinded and begging for death. With terrible and understated pity he leads him (as he pretends) to the edge of a cliff at Dover, lets him fall in a faint as if over the cliff, and discovers him alive as if at its foot. At no point in the scene does he reveal himself as his father's son. "Why I do trifle thus with his despair is done to cure it," he says. Perhaps our liturgies trifle, in order to cure it, with God's despair. Perhaps we are engaged in leading God to and through a mime of his own death, from which he will get up again grateful. Perhaps liturgy — a disguise we cannot yet put off — is grounded in what cannot be said, and its meaning always depends on what can be imagined.

Notes to Chapter 1

1. Richard Wilbur, *Conversations with Richard Wilbur* (Jackson: University Press of Mississippi, 1990), 35.
2. John of the Cross, *The Poems of Saint John of the Cross*, trans. Willis Barnstone (New York: New Directions, 1972), 84-85.
3. Ian Robinson, *Prayers for the New Babel: A Criticism of the Church of England Alternative Service Book 1980* ([Retford, Nottinghamshire]: Brynmill, 1983), 23.
4. Owen Barfield, *Saving the Appearances: A Study in Idolatry* (New York: Harcourt, Brace and World, 1965), 40-45.
5. Gershom G. Scholem, *On the Kabbalah and Its Symbolism*, trans. Ralph Mannheim (New York: Schocken, 1965), 15.
6. Rudolf Otto, *The Idea of the Holy*, trans. John W. Harvey, 2nd ed. (London: Oxford University Press, 1950), 60.
7. William James, *The Varieties of Religious Experience: A Study in Human Nature* (New York: Modern Library, [1936]), 46.
8. Ibid., 232.
9. Søren Kierkegaard, "Repetition," in *Fear and Trembling / Repetition*, ed. and trans. Howard V. Hong and Edna H. Hong (Princeton: Princeton University Press, 1983), 146.
10. William Blake, *Songs of Experience*.
11. William Wordsworth, *The Prelude*, Book 1, 392-93; the full story of the theft of the boat is told in lines 357-400.
12. Barfield, *Saving the Appearances*, 161.
13. Isa. 6:3, usually translated "the whole earth is full of his glory." *Kavod* implies gravity in both senses.
14. Exod. 3:14.
15. Eric Caplan, *From Ideology to Liturgy: Reconstructionist Worship and American Liberal Judaism* (Cincinnati: Hebrew Union College Press, 2002).
16. *The Book of Common Prayer* ([Greenwich, CT]: Seabury, 1979), 355; the older form can be found on 323 in what is now termed Rite I. The formula's prototype is in the opening lines of the Middle

English *The Cloud of Unknowing*; it underwent several permutations to arrive at the form it takes in Thomas Cranmer's 1549 *BCP*. From 1549 until 1979 only one change was made: "unto whom all hearts be open" was changed to "unto whom all hearts are open."

17. Heard in a motel near Nashville, May 2003.

18. Lavon Bayler, *Led by Love: Worship Resources for Year B* (Cleveland: United Church Press, 1996), 217.

19. Ibid., 205.

20. Miriam Therese Winter, *WomanPrayer, WomanSong: Resources for Ritual* (Oak Park, Ill.: Meyer-Stone, 1987), 107

21. *Musaf* (Additional) service for Rosh Hashanah and Yom Kippur; composite translation from several sources.

22. Stanley Rabinowitz, adapted by Shamai Kanter and Jack Riemer, in *Maḥzor for Rosh Hashanah and Yom Kippur: A Prayer Book for the Days of Awe*, ed. Jules Harlow, 2nd ed. (New York: The Rabbinical Assembly, 1978), 228.

23. Mordecai M. Kaplan, *Judaism as a Civilization: Toward a Reconstruction of American-Jewish Life* (New York: Macmillan, 1935).

24. *Siddur tefillot le-shabbat/Sabbath Prayer Book* [ed. Mordecai M. Kaplan and Eugene Kohn], (New York: The Jewish Reconstructionist Foundation, 1945), 114–115.

25. William Bright, "And now, O Father, mindful of the love," in *The Hymnal of the Protestant Episcopal Church in the United States of America 1940* (New York: The Church Pension Fund, 1943), Hymn 189 [n.p.].

26. Mark Twain, "The Intelligence of God."

27. Caplan, 147-49.

28. *Kol Haneshamah: Shabbat Veḥagim* [ed. David A. Teutsch], (Wyncote, Pa.: Reconstructionist Press, 1994), xi.

29. Ibid., 64, (emphasis added); this is from the *V'ahavta* paragraph of the *Shema Yisrael*, originally from Deut. 6:7.

30. Ibid., 96, from the fourth blessing of the Shabbat *Amidah*.

31. Ibid., 644.

32. *Sab'enu vaboker hasdekha*; the KJV has "O satisfy us early with thy mercy," a more literal translation except that *boker* is literally "morning."

33. Ibid., 192-94.

34. Ibid., 188, from Ps. 34.
35. Ibid., 216, from Ps. 122.
36. Richard Hirsh, "Spirituality and the Language of Prayer," *The Reconstructionist* 59 (Spring 1994), 24.
37. David Teutsch, "Seeking God in the Siddur: Reflections on *Kol Haneshamah*," *The Reconstructionist* 59 (Spring 1994), 14.
38. Isa. 45:7, as amended in the morning service (in the first blessing after the *Barekhu*) in every *siddur* I have seen.
39. Teutsch, 14 (emphasis in original).
40. Michael Signer, "The Poetics of Liturgy," in *The Changing Face of Jewish and Christian Worship in North America*, ed. Paul F. Bradshaw and Lawrence A. Hoffman (Notre Dame: University of Notre Dame Press, 1991), 186-187.
41. *Gates of Prayer: The New Union Prayerbook* (New York: Central Conference of American Rabbis, 1975), 625-626.
42. Signer, 188-89.
43. Thomas F. Merrill, "Sacred Parody and the Grammar of Devotion," *Criticism* (Sum. 1981), 205.
44. *Maḥzor for Rosh Hashanah and Yom Kippur*, 402.
45. Franz Rosenzweig, "The Secret of Biblical Narrative Form," in Martin Buber and Franz Rosenzweig, *Scripture and Translation*, trans. Lawrence Rosenwald with Everett Fox (Bloomington: Indiana University Press, 1994), 130.
46. Pirke Avot 1:14.
47. "A 'Fall to Freedom': The Immigrant's Lot is Not an Easy One," trans. and reprinted from *Der Stern*, Hamburg, in *World Press Review* 36 (Nov. 1989), 14.
48. J241.
49. J1286.

Notes to Chapter 2

1. Jean Piaget, *The Language and Thought of the Child,* trans Marjorie Gabain, (New York: New American Library, 1974), 31.
2. Lawrence Kohlberg, Judy Yaeger, and Else Hjertholm, "Private Speech: Four Studies and a Review of Theories," *Child Development* 39 (Sept. 1968), 703–704.

3. Vygotsky's second chapter particularly addresses this assumption of Piaget's.

4. Lev Vygotsky, *Thought and Language*, trans. and ed. Alex Kozulin (Cambridge, Mass: MIT Press, 1986), 232.

5. Ibid., 169.

6. Ibid., 228.

7. Ibid., 233.

8. Ibid., 83.

9. Ibid., 86.

10. Ibid., 228.

11. Ibid., 7-8.

12. Ibid., 10.

13. Wordsworth, *The Prelude*, Book 14, 226.

14. Vygotsky, 94.

15. Ibid., 182.

16. Kohlberg, Yaeger and Hjertholm, 715.

17. *BCP*, "A Prayer for All Conditions of Men," which entered the Anglican liturgy early and appears in most editions before the 1970s, in Morning and Evening Prayer before the General Thanksgiving.

18. Regrettably, I have been unable to retrace the source of this chant, which was given to me without attribution.

19. Ismar Elbogen, *Jewish Liturgy: A Comprehensive History*, trans. Raymonmd P. Scheindlin, ed. Joseph Heinemann, et. al. (Philadelphia, Pa.: Jewish Publication Society, 1993), 77–78, discusses the evolution of these blessings from a talmudic discussion of the pious Jew's morning activities, and some of the variant forms they have taken. The Orthodox *Complete Artscroll Siddur*, ed. Nosson Scherman (Brooklyn: Mesorah, 1986) and the Conservative *Siddur Sim Shalom* (New York: The Rabbinical Assembly, 2002) provide typical examples of the two approaches I have shown here.

20. Vygotsky, 31.

21. In many *siddurim* this is the closing prayer of the *Amidah*.

22. Matt. 6:11.

23. From the *Musaf* service on Yom Kippur, originally from Num. 6:24–26.

24. My translation, based on the text in *The Metsudah Machzor*, ed. Avrohom Davis (New York: Metsudah, 1985), 611-13.

25. Elbogen, 64.

26. 1 Cor. 15:42-53, KJV.

27. Alex Kozulin in his introduction to Vygotsky, xxxvii.

28. Frits Staal, "The Meaninglessness of Ritual," *Numen* 26, Fasc. 1 (June 1979), 3.

29. Ibid., 9.

30. Ibid., 21.

31. David Crystal, *The English Tone of Voice: Essays in Intonation, Prosody and Paralanguage* (London: Edward Arnold, 1975), 102.

32. Ibid., 102.

33. Staal, 19.

34. Vygotsky, 91.

35. Kohlberg, Yaeger and Hjertholm, 696.

36. A term I owe to Sarah Thomson.

37. Steven Pinker, *Words and Rules: The Ingredients of Language* (New York: Basic Books, 1999), 81-82.

38. *Kol Haneshamah* uses this formula in the morning blessings (153–161).

39. Pinker, 82.

40. Margaret A. Roche, "Hammond Song," *The Roches* (Warner Brothers BSK 3298, 1979). © 1971 ASCAP.

41. John J. Ratey, *A User's Guide to the Brain: Perception, Attention, and the Four Theaters of the Brain* (New York: Vintage, 2001), 5.

42. Donald Davidson, "What Metaphors Mean," in *On Metaphor*, ed. Sheldon Sacks (Chicago: University of Chicago Press, 1979), 29.

43. Ted Cohen, "Metaphor and the Cultivation of Intimacy," in *On Metaphor*, ed. Sheldon Sacks (Chicago: University of Chicago Press, 1979), 6.

44. Ibid., 9-10.

45. Paul Ricoeur, "The Metaphorical Process as Cognition, Imagination, and Feeling," in *On Metaphor*, ed. Sheldon Sacks (Chicago: University of Chicago Press, 1979), 154.

46. Otto, 42.

47. Elias Canetti, *The Human Province*, trans. Joachim Neugroschel (New York: Farrar Straus Giroux, 1978), 2.

48. Otto, 45.

49. Israel Scheffler, *Inquiries: Philosophical Studies of Language, Sci-*

ence, and Learning (Indianapolis: Hackett, 1986), 353 (emphasis in original).

50. Mark Johnson, *Moral Imagination: Implications of Cognitive Science for Ethics* (Chicago: University of Chicago Press, 1993), 58 (emphasis in original).
51. Ibid., 165.
52. Ibid., 168-171.
53. Ibid., 33.
54. Ibid., 194.
55. Scheffler, 50.
56. Ratey, 34-39, 277-8, 363-68.
57. Isa. 42:14.
58. Bertolt Brecht, "Short Description of a New Technique of Acting which Produces an Alienation Effect," in *Brecht on Theatre: The Development of an Aesthetic*, ed. and trans. John Willett (New York: Hill and Wang, 1992), 143-44.
59. Brecht, 99, editor's note.
60. Victor Shklovsky, "Art as Technique," in *Russian Formalist Criticism: Four Essays*, trans. Lee T. Lemon and Marion J. Reis (Lincoln: University of Nebraska Press, 1965), 6.
61. Ibid., 12 (final emphasis added).
62. Ibid., 24. In this connection, William H. McNeill's *Keeping Together in Time: Dance and Drill in Human History* (Cambridge, Mass.: Harvard University Press, 1995) is an interesting discussion of the convergence of physiology and psychology in rhythmical and unison body movements. It is also worth observing that free verse, now that it has become a convention and not a novelty, is as unremarkable as nineteenth-century doggerel; as with any poetic form, when it succeeds it succeeds on the strength of the poet's skill and imagination, not on its formal characteristics.
63. Ibid., 16.
64. James, 150.
65. Ibid., 149.
66. Isak Dinesen, "The Dreamers," in *Seven Gothic Tales* (New York: Harrison Smith and Robert Haas, 1934), 275.
67. Arthur J. Deikman, "Deautomatization and the Mystic Experience," in *Altered States of Consciousness: A Book of Readings*, ed.

Charles T. Tart (New York: Wiley, 1969), 38.

68. Matt. 18:3.

Notes to Chapter 3

1. Ratey, 114.
2. Ibid., 121.
3. Isa. 40:2.
4. Ratey, 186.
5. Shakespeare, Richard II, 2.1.5-6.
6. For Tyndale, see David Daniell, *William Tyndale: A Biography* (New Haven: Yale University Press, 1994). For Cranmer, see Diarmaid MacCulloch, *Thomas Cranmer: A Life* (New Haven: Yale University Press, 1996). For Coverdale, see David Daniell, *The Bible in English: Its History and Influence* (New Haven: Yale University Press, 2003), 176-78, 209-18.
7. Franz Rosenzweig, "Scripture and Luther," in Buber and Rosenzweig, *Scripture and Translation*, 49.
8. Daniell, *William Tyndale* 79.
9. Ibid., 285.
10. Jon Nielson and Royal Skousen, "How Much of the King James Bible is William Tyndale's?: An Estimation Based on Sampling," *Reformation* 3 (1998): 49-74. To be precise, the answer is 83.7 percent of the New Testament and 75.7 percent of the books of the Hebrew Bible that Tyndale lived to translate.
11. Daniell, *William Tyndale* 14.
12. John 14:1.
13. Daniell, *William Tyndale* 137.
14. Quoted in Willis Barnstone, *The New Covenant, Commonly Called the New Testament. Volume 1: The Four Gospels and Apocalypse* (New York: Riverhead, 2002), 206.
15. Canetti, 11.
16. Jan Freeman, "Talking through the terror," *Boston Globe* 16 September 2001, D8.
17. John Bradford, quoted in J. W. Blench, *Preaching in England in the late 15th and 16th Centuries* (New York: Barnes and Noble, 1964), 265.

18. William Tyndale, *The Obedience of a Christian Man*, ed. David Daniell (London: Penguin, 2000), 108–9.

19. Ibid., 163–64.

20. Shakespeare, *King Lear* 2.2.64–69.

21. MacCulloch, 439.

22. Thomas Cranmer, *Miscellaneous Writings and Letters*, ed. John Edmund Cox (Cambridge: Cambridge University Press, 1846), 225.

23. Shakespeare, *The Tempest* 4.1.199.

24. Shakespeare, *King Lear* 3.7.64.

25. Walter J. Ong, *Orality and Literacy: The Technologizing of the Word* (London: Routledge, 1982), 34.

26. Ibid., 35-36. Tolstoy's peasant Platon in War and Peace, whose luminous gentleness is so transformative to Pierre in his experience as a prisoner of war, speaks almost entirely in proverbs: "Suffer an hour, live an age," "The worm nibbles the cabbage, but dies before it's done," "A promise is kin to the deed." For Platon one proverb may be interchangeable with another, so that when Pierre asks him to repeat one he offers something else in its place; his train of thought meanders, even among memorable thoughts.

27. Shakespeare, *King Lear* 3.3.106–7.

28. Shakespeare, *Romeo and Juliet* 2.2.43–44.

29. Ong, *Orality and Literacy* 7–8.

30. Ibid., 78.

31. Ibid., 178–179.

32. Ibid., 8.

33. Ibid., 34.

34. Desiderius Erasmus, *On Copia of Words and Ideas*, trans. Donald B. King and H. David Rix (Milwaukee: Marquette University Press, 1963), 39–42.

35. Walter J. Ong, *Ramus, Method, and the Decay of Dialogue* (Cambridge, MA: Harvard University Press, 1958), 211.

36. Erasmus, 30.

37. Ong, *Orality and Literacy* 111.

38. Ibid., 44.

39. Matt. 5:38–39.

40. Luke 4:20–21.

41. See Charles Barber, *Early Modern English* (Edinburgh: Edinburgh

University Press, 1997).

42. Morris W. Croll, *Style, Rhetoric and Rhythm: Essays by Morris W. Croll*, ed. J. Max Patrick et al. (Princeton: Princeton University Press, 1966), 185.

43. Daniell, *William Tyndale* 290.

44. Croll, 95.

45. Ibid., 210 (emphasis in original).

46. Ibid., 199.

47. Ibid., 231–232.

48. Ibid., 199.

49. Ian Robinson, *The Establishment of Modern English Prose in the Reformation and the Enlightenment* (Cambridge: Cambridge University Press, 1998), 20–34.

50. Croll, 232.

51. Ong, *Ramus* 188.

52. Ibid., 192.

53. Ibid., 213.

54. Ibid., 212.

55. Piaget, 148–170.

56. Ong, *Ramus* 287.

57. Croll, 232.

58. Francis Bacon, "Of the Advancement of Learning," in *The Philosophical Works of Francis Bacon*, ed. John M. Robertson (London: Routledge, 1905), 125.

59. Stanley E. Fish, *Self-Consuming Artifacts: The Experience of Seventeenth-Century Literature* (Berkeley: University of California Press, 1972), 378.

60. Ibid., 1-2.

61. Ibid., 8.

62. I discovered these lines twenty-five years ago or so, and have been unable to retrace their source; I would expect to find the verse in one of Eleanour Sinclair Rohde's herbals, but so far have not. On the Internet it is quoted without attribution on an anonymous neopagan website.

63. Fish, 3.

64. John Dryden, *Absalom and Achitophel* 1.163–164.

65. Fish, 380.

66. Owen Barfield, *Poetic Diction* (Middletown, CT: Wesleyan University Press, 1973), 154 (emphasis added).
67. T. S. Eliot, "The Metaphysical Poets," in *Selected Essays, 1917-1932* (New York: Harcourt, Brace, 1932), 247.
68. Robinson, *Establishment of Modern English Prose* 164.
69. George Steiner, "Linguistics and Poetics," in *Extraterritorial: Papers on Literature and the Language Revolution* (London: Faber, 1972), 131-32.
70. Edward Harwood, *A Liberal Translation of the New Testament; Being an Attempt to Translate the Sacred Writings with the same Freedom, Spirit, and Elegance, with which Other English Translations from the Greek Classics have lately been executed [...] with Select Notes, Critical and Explanatory*, 1768, qtd. in Daniell, *Bible* 606-17.
71. Ibid., 614.
72. Luke 15:20.
73. Daniell, *Bible* 607.
74. Gen. 22:8.
75. James Hervey, *Meditations and Contemplations* (New York: Robert Carter and Brothers, 1851), 274-75 (originally published 1747).
76. Christopher Smart, *The Poetical Works of Christopher Smart*, ed. Karina Williamson (Oxford: Clarendon Press, 1980), vol. 1: Jubilate Agno, fragment B, line 42, p. 19.
77. Ibid., fragment B, line 22, p. 15.
78. Ibid., fragment B, line 305, p. 61.
79. Ibid., fragment B, line 1, p. 12.
80. Harold Bloom, introduction to *The Literary Criticism of John Ruskin* (New York: Da Capo, 1965), xxiii.
81. T. S. Eliot, 248.
82. Jonathan Bate, *Romantic Ecology: Wordsworth and the Environmental Tradition* (London: Routledge, 1991), 31, with relevant discussion on 22-26.
83. William Blake, *The Marriage of Heaven and Hell*, Plate 5.
84. John Ruskin, *Modern Painters 5*, Part 8, Chapter 4.
85. Ong, *Orality and Literacy* 160.
86. Robinson, *Establishment of Modern English Prose* 164-65.
87. George Steiner, "The Distribution of Discourse," in *On Difficulty*

and Other Essays (New York: Oxford University Press, 1978), 84-85.

88. Jane Austen, *Sense and Sensibility*, Chapter 46.

89. George Eliot, *Daniel Deronda*, Chapter 22.

90. Ong, *Orality and Literacy* 136-37.

91. *BCP* [1928], General Confession in the Communion service.

92. Ibid., Prayer for All Conditions of Men.

93. Ibid., in one of several Collects in the Prayers and Thanksgivings section following Morning and Evening Prayer.

94. Ibid., Collect for 4th Sunday after Epiphany.

95. Ibid., Prayers and Thanksgivings section.

96. Ibid., Collect for 4th Sunday after Trinity.

97. B. Dowe and F. McNaughton, "Rivers of Babylon," Ackee Music 1982, on Jimmy Cliff, *The Harder They Come* (Mango MLPS-9202).

98. Steiner, "Linguistics and Poetics" 129.

Notes to Chapter 4

1. *BCP* 1979, 95.

2. Shakespeare, *King Lear* 1.1.87.

3. James, 492.

4. Lam. R., Introduction 24.

5. Maya Angelou, *I Know Why the Caged Bird Sings* (New York: Bantam, 1971), 69-74.

6. Piaget, Chapter 3, 93-139.

7. Elaine Scarry, *The Body in Pain: The Making and Unmaking of the World* (New York: Oxford University Press, 1985), 4.

8. Peter Shabad, "The Most Intimate of Creations: Symptoms as Memorials to One's Lonely Suffering," in *Symbolic Loss: The Ambiguity of Mourning and Memory at Century's End*, ed. Peter Homans (Charlottesville: University Press of Virginia, 2000), 200.

9. Jerome Groopman, "The Grief Industry," *The New Yorker*, 26 Jan. 2004, 32.

10. Shabad, 210.

11. Ratey, 211.

12. Ibid., 210.

13. Ibid., 269.
14. Scarry, 6.
15. Carol Doran and Thomas H. Troeger, *New Hymns for the Life of the Church: To Make Our Prayer and Music One* (New York: Oxford University Press, 1992), 43.
16. Doran and Troeger, 56.
17. Anna Wierzbicka, *Emotions Across Languages and Cultures: Diversity and Universals* (Cambridge: Cambridge University Press, 1999), 3.
18. Ibid., 32.
19. Ibid., 26–27.
20. Ibid., 123–167.
21. Shakespeare, *A Winter's Tale* 3.ii.217–19.
22. Austen, Chapter 37.
23. Murray Cox and Alice Theilgaard, *Mutative Metaphors in Psychotherapy: The Aeolian Mode* (London: Tavistock, 1987), 104.
24. Mark B. Evans, "The Role of Metaphor in Psychotherapy and Personality Change: A Theoretical Reformulation," *Psychotherapy* 25 (Winter 1988), 549.
25. Cox and Theilgaard, 84.
26. Evans, 550.
27. Lynne E. Angus and David L. Rennie, "Therapist Participation in Metaphor Generation: Collaborative and Noncollaborative Styles," *Psychotherapy* 25 (Winter 1988), 556–58.
28. Evans, 550.
29. Cox and Theilgaard, 72 (emphasis in original).
30. Ibid., 79.
31. Ibid., 149.
32. Ibid., 140.
33. Ibid., 147–148.
34. Ibid., 147.
35. Stephen Prickett, *Words and* The Word: *Language, Poetics and Biblical Interpretation* (Cambridge: Cambridge University Press, 1986), 236 (emphasis in original).
36. Ibid.
37. Ibid., 9.
38. Ibid., 10 (emphasis in original).

39. Steiner, "The Distribution of Discourse," 90.

40. Andrew Shanks, *"What is Truth?": Towards a Theological Poetics* (London: Routledge, 2001), 9–15.

41. Ibid., 144.

42. Ibid., 72 (emphasis in original).

43. Ibid., 8.

44. Ibid., 15.

45. Ibid., 20–21.

46. Milan Kundera, *The Unbearable Lightness of Being*, trans. Michael Henry Heim (New York: Harper, 1991), 251.

47. Shanks, 69.

48. Richard A. Cohen, "Introduction: For the Unforeseeable Future," in Emmanuel Levinas, *Unforeseen History*, trans. Nidra Poller (Urbana: University of Chicago Press, 2004), xxiii.

49. A useful discussion of this phenomenon is Tomaś Kulka, *Kitsch and Art* (University Park, Pa.: Pennsylvania State University Press, 1996).

50. Kundera, 248.

51. Ibid., 253.

52. Ibid., 250.

53. Joseph Boucher, personal communication, 17 July 2003.

54. Scarry, 171 (emphasis in original).

55. Peter Brook, *The Empty Space* (London: MacGibbon and Kee, 1968), 111–112.

56. James, 46–47.

57. George Steiner, *Real Presences* (Chicago: University of Chicago Press, 1989), 224.

58. James, 159.

59. Emmanuel Levinas, *Otherwise than Being, or Beyond Essence*, trans. Alphonso Lingis (Pittsburgh: Duquesne University Press, 1998), 49.

60. Abraham J. Heschel, *The Prophets: An Introduction*, vol. 1 (New York: Harper Colophon, 1962), 9.

61. Levinas, *Otherwise than Being*, 56–57.

62. George Steiner, *In Bluebeard's Castle: Some Notes towards the Redefinition of Culture* (New Haven: Yale University Press, 1971), 36.

63. Ibid., 44.

64. John Donne, *Divine Meditations* 14 (spelling and punctuation modernized).

65. Slavoj Žižek and Glyn Daly, eds. *Conversations with Slavoj Žižek* (Cambridge: Polity, 2004), 59.

66. C. S. Lewis, *That Hideous Strength*, Chapter 15.

67. Žižek, 59.

68. The entire second part of Scarry's *The Body in Pain* is devoted to this question; see especially 161-80, 243-56, 281-293. "A chair, as though it were itself put in pain, as though it knew from the inside the problem of body weight, will only then accommodate and eliminate the problem" (288). "If one imagines one human being seeing another human being in pain, one human being perceiving in another discomfort and in the same moment wishing the other to be relieved of the discomfort, something in that fraction of a second is occurring inside the first person's brain involving the complex action of many neurons that is, importantly, not just a perception of an actuality...but an alteration of that actuality.... The shape of the chair is not the shape of the skeleton, the shape of body weight, nor even the shape of pain-perceived, but the shape of perceived-pain-wished-gone" (289–90).

69. Jacob Neusner, *The Enchantments of Judaism: Rites of Transformation from Birth through Death* (New York: Basic Books, 1987), 3–7.

70. Donald Kalsched, *The Inner World of Trauma: Archetypal Defenses of the Personal Spirit* (London: Routledge, 1996), 146.

71. Lancelot Andrewes, *The Private Devotions of Lancelot Andrewes* (Preces Privatae), ed. and trans. by F. E. Brightman (Gloucester, Mass.: Peter Smith, 1983), 31.

Notes to Chapter 5

1. Steiner, "The Distribution of Discourse" 92.

2. Angus and Rennie, 559.

3. Num. 24:5.

4. Lam. 5:21, used at the conclusion of the Torah service.

5. Attributed to Mark Strand by Anthony Hecht, "Paralipomena to *The Hidden Law*," in *Sewanee Writers on Writing*, ed. Wyatt Prunty

(Baton Rouge: Louisiana State University Press, 2000), 64.

6. Vienna Cobb Anderson, *Prayers of Our Hearts in Word and Action* (New York: Crossroad, 1991), xi.

7. Jer. 20:7, as translated and discussed by Heschel, vol. 1, 113–114.

8. Anderson, xi.

9. *Out of the Depths I Call to You: A Book of Prayers for the Married Jewish Woman* [*Seder tefilot nidah, halah, hadlakah*], ed. and trans. Nina Beth Cardin (Northvale, NJ: Jason Aronson, 1995), 38-53.

10. Ibid., 45 (Ps. 17:8).

11. Ibid., 47 (Ps. 121:1, 6).

12. Ibid., 48 (Ps. 91:5).

13. Ibid., 53 (Ps. 23:4, 5).

14. Tikva Frymer-Kensky, *Motherprayer: The Pregnant Woman's Spiritual Companion* (New York: Riverhead, 1995), 226 (Ps. 116:9).

15. Ibid., 227 (Ps. 118:19).

16. Mishnah Berakhot 9:5.

17. Gen. R. 9:7.

18. Doran and Troeger, 28.

19. Blake, *Marriage of Heaven and Hell*, Plate 8.

20. Ian Robinson, *The Survival of English: Essays in the Criticism of Language* (Cambridge: Cambridge University Press, 1973), 225.

21. Zohar I, 244b.

22. Blake, *Marriage of Heaven and Hell*, Plates 12-13 (spelling and punctuation modernized).

23. Harold M. Schulweis, *Evil and the Morality of God* (Cincinnati: Hebrew Union College Press, 1984).

24. Scarry, 221-22.

25. Ibid., 323.

26. Blake, *Laocoön*.

Alter, Robert, trans. *The Five Books of Moses: A Translation with Commentary.* New York: Norton, 2004.

Anderson, Vienna Cobb. *Prayers of Our Hearts in Word and Action.* New York: Crossroad, 1991.

Andrewes, Lancelot. *The Private Devotions of Lancelot Andrewes* (Preces Privatae). Trans. and ed. by F. E. Brightman. Gloucester, Mass.: Peter Smith, 1983.

Angelou, Maya. *I Know Why the Caged Bird Sings.* New York: Bantam, 1971.

Angus, Lynne E., and David L. Rennie. "Therapist Participation in Metaphor Generation: Collaborative and Noncollaborative Styles." *Psychotherapy* 25 (Winter 1988): 552-60.

Bacon, Francis. "Of the Advancement of Learning." In *The Philosophical Works of Francis Bacon.* Ed. John M. Robertson. London: Routledge, 1905.

Barber, Charles. *Early Modern English.* Edinburgh: Edinburgh University Press, 1997.

Barfield, Owen. *Poetic Diction.* Middletown, CT: Wesleyan University Press, 1973.

———. *Saving the Appearances: A Study in Idolatry.* New York: Harcourt, Brace and World, 1965.

Barnstone, Willis, trans. *The New Covenant, Commonly Called the New Testament. Volume 1: The Four Gospels and Apocalypse.* New York: Riverhead, 2002.

Bate, Jonathan. *Romantic Ecology: Wordsworth and the Environmental Tradition.* London: Routledge, 1991.

Bayler, Lavon. *Led by Love: Worship Resources for Year B.* Cleveland: United Church Press, 1996.

Blench, J. W. *Preaching in England in the late 15th and 16th Centuries.* New York: Barnes and Noble, 1964.

Blumenthal, David. *Facing the Abusing God: A Theology of Protest.* Louisville: Westminster/John Knox Press, 1993.

The Book of Common Prayer, Administration of the Sacraments and Other Rites and Ceremonies of the Church: According to the Use of the Protestant Episcopal Church in the United States of America: Together with The Psalter of Psalms of David. New York: The Church Pension Fund, 1945 [1928 ed.].

The Book of Common Prayer, and Administration of the Sacraments and Other Rites and Ceremonies of the Church, Together with The Psalter of Psalms of David: According to the use of The Episcopal Church. [Greenwich, CT]: Seabury, 1979.

Brecht, Bertolt. *Brecht on Theatre: The Development of an Aesthetic.* Ed. and trans. John Willett. New York: Hill and Wang, 1992.

Brook, Peter. *The Empty Space.* London: MacGibbon and Kee, 1968.

Buber, Martin, and Franz Rosenzweig, *Scripture and Translation.* Trans. Lawrence Rosenwald with Everett Fox. Bloomington: Indiana University Press, 1994.

Canetti, Elias. *The Human Province.* Trans. Joachim Neugroschel. New York: Farrar Straus Giroux, 1978.

Caplan, Eric. *From Ideology to Liturgy: Reconstructionist Worship and American Liberal Judaism.* Cincinnati: Hebrew Union College Press, 2002.

The Cloud of Unknowing, and The Book of Privy Counseling. Ed. Phyllis Hodgson. London: Oxford University Press, for the Early English Text Society, 1944.

Cohen, Leonard. *Book of Mercy.* New York: Villard, 1984. Most of the contents reprinted in *Stranger Music: Selected Poems and Songs.* New York: Pantheon, 1993.

Cohen, Ted. "Metaphor and the Cultivation of Intimacy." In *On Metaphor*. Ed. Sheldon Sacks. Chicago: University of Chicago Press, 1979, 1-10.

Cox, Murray, and Alice Theilgaard. *Mutative Metaphors in Psychotherapy: The Aeolian Mode*. London: Tavistock, 1987.

Cranmer, Thomas. *Miscellaneous Writings and Letters*. Ed. John Edmund Cox. Cambridge: Cambridge University Press, 1846.

Croll, Morris W. *Style, Rhetoric and Rhythm: Essays by Morris W. Croll*. Ed. J. Max Patrick et al. Princeton: Princeton University Press, 1966.

Crystal, David. *The English Tone of Voice: Essays in Intonation, Prosody and Paralanguage*. London: Edward Arnold, 1975.

Daniell, David. *The Bible in English: Its History and Influence*. New Haven: Yale University Press, 2003.

———. *William Tyndale: A Biography*. New Haven: Yale University Press, 1994.

Davidson, Donald. "What Metaphors Mean." In *On Metaphor*. Ed. Sheldon Sacks. Chicago: University of Chicago Press, 1979, 29-45.

Deikman, Arthur J. "Deautomatization and the Mystic Experience." In *Altered States of Consciousness: A Book of Readings*. Ed. Charles T. Tart. New York: Wiley, 1969: 23-43.

Dinesen, Isak. "The Dreamers." In *Seven Gothic Tales*. New York: Harrison Smith and Robert Haas, 1934.

Doran, Carol, and Thomas H. Troeger. *New Hymns for the Life of the Church: To Make Our Prayer and Music One*. New York: Oxford University Press, 1992.

Elbogen, Ismar. *Jewish Liturgy: A Comprehensive History*. Ed. Joseph Heinemann, et. al. Trans. Raymond P. Scheindlin. Philadelphia: Jewish Publication Society, 1993.

Eliot, T. S. "The Metaphysical Poets." In *Selected Essays, 1917-1932*. New York: Harcourt, Brace, 1932: 241-50.

Erasmus, Desiderius. *On Copia of Words and Ideas*. Trans. Donald B. King and H. David Rix. Milwaukee: Marquette University Press, 1963.

Evans, Mark B. "The Role of Metaphor in Psychotherapy and Personality Change: A Theoretical Reformulation." *Psychotherapy* 25 (Winter 1988): 543-51.

Falk, Marcia. *The Book of Blessings: New Jewish Prayers for Daily Life, the Sabbath, and the New Moon Festival. Sefer Habrakhot: Siddur b'girsah ḥadashah limot haḥol, l'shabbat, ul'rosh ḥodesh*. San Francisco: Harper, 1996.

"A 'Fall to Freedom': The Immigrant's Lot is Not an Easy One." Trans. and reprinted from *Der Stern*, Hamburg, in *World Press Review* 36 (Nov. 1989): 13-14.

The First and Second Prayer Books of Edward VI. London: J. M. Dent and Sons, 1910. Reprinted 1960.

Fisch, Harold, ed. and trans. *Torah Neviim Ketuvim: The Holy Scriptures*. Jerusalem: Koren, 1977.

Fish, Stanley E. *Self-Consuming Artifacts: The Experience of Seventeenth-Century Literature*. Berkeley: University of California Press, 1972.

Fox, Everett, trans. *The Five Books of Moses: Genesis, Exodus, Leviticus, Numbers, Deuteronomy: A New Translation with Introductions, Commentary, and Notes*. New York: Schocken, 1995.

Freeman, Jan. "Talking through the terror." *Boston Globe* 16 September 2001: D8.

Frymer-Kensky, Tikva. *Motherprayer: The Pregnant Woman's Spiritual Companion*. New York: Riverhead, 1995.

Gates of Prayer: The New Union Prayerbook. New York: Central Conference of American Rabbis, 1975.

Groopman, Jerome. "The Grief Industry." *The New Yorker*, 26 Jan. 2004: 30-38.

Hecht, Anthony. "Paralipomena to The Hidden Law." In *Sewanee Writers on Writing*. Ed. Wyatt Prunty. Baton Rouge: Louisiana State University Press, 2000.

Herman, Judith. *Trauma and Recovery*. New York: Basic Books, 1997.

Hervey, James. *Meditations and Contemplations*. New York: Robert Carter and Brothers, 1851 (originally published 1747).

Heschel, Abraham J. *The Prophets: An Introduction*. New York: Harper Colophon, 1962.

Hirsh, Richard. "Spirituality and the Language of Prayer." *The Reconstructionist* 59:1 (Spring 1994): 21-26.

Hyde, Lewis. *The Gift: Imagination and the Erotic Life of Property*. New York: Random House, 1983.

James, William. *The Varieties of Religious Experience: A Study in Human Nature*. New York: Modern Library, [1936].

John of the Cross. *The Poems of Saint John of the Cross*. Trans. Willis Barnstone. New York: New Directions, 1972.

Johnson, Mark. *Moral Imagination: Implications of Cognitive Science for Ethics*. Chicago: University of Chicago Press, 1993.

Kalsched, Donald. *The Inner World of Trauma: Archetypal Defenses of the Personal Spirit*. London: Routledge, 1996.

Kaplan, Mordecai M. *Judaism as a Civilization: Toward a Reconstruction of American-Jewish Life*. New York: Macmillan, 1935.

Kierkegaard, Søren. "Repetition." In *Fear and Trembling / Repetition*. Ed. and trans. Howard V. Hong and Edna H. Hong. Princeton: Princeton University Press, 1983.

Kohlberg, Lawrence, Judy Yaeger, and Else Hjertholm. "Private Speech: Four Studies and a Review of Theories." *Child Development* 39: 691-736, Sept. 1968.

Kol Haneshamah: Shabbat Veḥagim. Ed. David A. Teutsch. Wyncote, Pa.: The Reconstructionist Press, 1994.

Korsak, Mary Phil, trans. *At the Start...Genesis Made New.* Louvain: Leuvense Schrijversaktie, 1992.

Kulka, Tomaś. *Kitsch and Art.* University Park, Pa.: Pennsylvania State University Press, 1996.

Kundera, Milan. *The Unbearable Lightness of Being.* Trans. Michael Henry Heim. New York: Harper, 1991.

Levinas, Emmanuel. *Otherwise than Being, or Beyond Essence.* Trans. Alphonso Lingis. Pittsburgh: Duquesne University Press, 1998.

————. *Unforeseen History.* Trans. Nidra Poller. Urbana: University of Chicago Press, 2004.

MacCulloch, Diarmaid. *Thomas Cranmer: A Life.* New Haven: Yale University Press, 1996.

Maḥzor for Rosh Hashanah and Yom Kippur: A Prayer Book for the Days of Awe. Ed. Jules Harlow. Second edition. New York: The Rabbinical Assembly, 1978.

McNeill, William H. *Keeping Together in Time: Dance and Drill in Human History.* Cambridge, Mass.: Harvard University Press, 1995.

Merrill, Thomas F. "Sacred Parody and the Grammar of Devotion." *Criticism* (Sum. 1981): 195-210.

The Metsudah Machzor. Ed. Avrohom Davis. New York: Metsudah, 1985.

Mitchell, Stephen, trans. *The Book of Job.* San Francisco: North Point Press, 1987.

Morley, Janet. *All Desires Known.* Expanded ed. Harrisburg, PA: Morehouse, 1992.

Neusner, Jacob. *The Enchantments of Judaism: Rites of Transformation from Birth through Death.* New York: Basic Books, 1987.

The New Mahzor for Rosh Hashanah and Yom Kippur. Ed. Sidney Greenberg and Jonathan D. Levine. Rev. and expanded ed. Bridgeport, CT: The Prayer Book Press, 1978.

Nielson, Jon, and Royal Skousen. "How Much of the King James Bible is William Tyndale's?: An Estimation Based on Sampling." *Reformation* 3 (1998): 49-74.

On Metaphor. Ed. Sheldon Sacks. Chicago: University of Chicago Press, 1979.

Ong, Walter J. *Orality and Literacy: The Technologizing of the Word.* London: Routledge, 1982.

————. *Ramus, Method, and the Decay of Dialogue.* Cambridge, MA: Harvard University Press, 1958.

Otto, Rudolf. *The Idea of the Holy.* Trans. John W. Harvey. 2nd ed. London: Oxford University Press, 1950.

Out of the Depths I Call to You: A Book of Prayers for the Married Jewish Woman [*Seder tefilot nidah, halah, hadlakah*]. Ed. and trans. Nina Beth Cardin. Northvale, NJ: Jason Aronson, 1995.

Piaget, Jean. *The Language and Thought of the Child.* Trans. Marjorie Gabain.New York: New American Library, 1974.

Pinker, Steven. *Words and Rules: The Ingredients of Language.* New York: Basic Books, 1999.

Price, Reynolds, trans. *A Palpable God: Thirty Stories Translated from the Bible with an Essay on the Origins and Life of Narrative.* San Francisco: North Point Press, 1985.

————, trans. *Three Gospels.* New York: Scribner, 1996.

Prickett, Stephen. *Words and* The Word: *Language, Poetics and Biblical Interpretation.* Cambridge: Cambridge University Press, 1986.

Ratey, John J. *A User's Guide to the Brain: Perception, Attention, and the Four Theaters of the Brain.* New York: Vintage, 2001.

Ricoeur, Paul. "The Metaphorical Process as Cognition, Imagination, and Feeling." In *On Metaphor.* Ed. Sheldon Sacks. Chicago: University of Chicago Press, 1979, 141-157.

Robinson, Ian. *The Establishment of Modern English Prose in the Reformation and the Enlightenment.* Cambridge: Cambridge University Press, 1998.

————. *Prayers for the New Babel: A Criticism of the Church of England Alternative Service Book 1980.* [Retford, Nottinghamshire]: Brynmill, 1983.

————. *The Survival of English: Essays in the Criticism of Language.* Cambridge: Cambridge University Press, 1973.

Rosenzweig, Franz. "The Secret of Biblical Narrative Form." In *Martin Buber and Franz Rosenzweig, Scripture and Translation.* Tr. Lawrence Rosenwald with Everett Fox. Bloomington: Indiana University Press, 1994: 129-142.

Roskies, David. *Night Words: A Midrash on the Holocaust.* Washington, DC: B'nai B'rith Hillel Foundations, 1971.

Ruskin, John. *The Literary Criticism of John Ruskin.* Ed. Harold Bloom. New York: Da Capo, 1965.

Scarry, Elaine. *The Body in Pain: The Making and Unmaking of the World.* New York: Oxford University Press, 1985.

Scheffler, Israel. *Inquiries: Philosophical Studies of Language, Science, and Learning.* Indianapolis: Hackett, 1986.

Scholem, Gershom G. *On the Kabbalah and Its Symbolism.* Trans. Ralph Mannheim. New York: Schocken, 1965.

Shabad, Peter. "The Most Intimate of Creations: Symptoms as Memorials to One's Lonely Suffering." In *Symbolic Loss: The Ambiguity of Mourning and Memory at Century's End.* Ed. Peter Homans. Charlottesville: University Press of Virginia, 2000, 197-212.

Shanks, Andrew. *"What is Truth?": Towards a Theological Poetics.* London: Routledge, 2001.

Shklovsky, Victor. "Art as Technique." In *Russian Formalist Criticism: Four Essays*, trans. Lee T. Lemon and Marion J. Reis. Lincoln: University of Nebraska Press, 1965, 3-24.

Siddur tefillot le-shabbat/Sabbath Prayer Book. Ed. Mordecai M. Kaplan and Eugene Kohn. New York: The Jewish Reconstructionist Foundation, 1945.

Signer, Michael. "The Poetics of Liturgy." In *The Changing Face of Jewish and Christian Worship in North America.* Ed. Paul F. Bradshaw and Lawrence A. Hoffman. Notre Dame: University of Notre Dame Press, 1991:184-198.

Smart, Christopher. *The Poetical Works of Christopher Smart.* Ed. Karina Williamson. Vol. 1: Jubilate Agno. Oxford: Clarendon Press, 1980.

Staal, Frits. "The Meaninglessness of Ritual." *Numen* 26, Fasc. 1, June 1979: 2-22.

Steiner, George. "The Distribution of Discourse." In *On Difficulty and Other Essays.* New York: Oxford University Press, 1978, 48-94.

————. *In Bluebeard's Castle: Some Notes towards the Redefinition of Culture.* New Haven: Yale University Press, 1971.

————. "Linguistics and Poetics." In *Extraterritorial: Papers on Literature and the Language Revolution.* London: Faber, 1972: 126-154.

————. *Real Presences.* Chicago: University of Chicago Press, 1989.

Stien, Phyllis T., and Joshua Kendall. *Psychological Trauma and the Developing Brain: Neurologically Based Interventions for Troubled Children.* New York: Haworth, 2004.

Teutsch, David. "Seeking God in the Siddur: Reflections on *Kol Haneshamah.*" *The Reconstructionist* 59:1 (Spring 1994): 12-20.

Tyndale, William. *The Obedience of a Christian Man.* Ed. David Daniell. London: Penguin, 2000.

——, trans. *Tyndale's New Testament: Translated from the Greek by William Tyndale in 1534.* Ed. David Daniell. New Haven: Yale University Press, 1989.

——, trans. *Tyndale's Old Testament: Being the Pentateuch of 1530, Joshua to 2 Chronicles of 1537, and Jonah.* Ed. David Daniell. New Haven: Yale University Press, 1992.

Vygotsky, Lev. *Thought and Language.* Trans. and ed. Alex Kozulin. Cambridge, Mass.: MIT Press, 1986.

Wierzbicka, Anna. *Emotions across Languages and Cultures: Diversity and Universals.* Cambridge: Cambridge University Press, 1999.

Wieseltier, Leon. *Kaddish.* New York: Knopf, 1998.

Wilbur, Richard. *Conversations with Richard Wilbur.* Jackson: University Press of Mississippi, 1990.

Winter, Miriam Therese. *WomanPrayer, WomanSong: Resources for Ritual.* Oak Park, Ill.: Meyer-Stone, 1987.

Žižek, Slavoj, and Glyn Daly, *Conversations with Slavoj Žižek.* Cambridge: Polity, 2004.

Made in the USA
Lexington, KY
26 November 2010